PRESSURE COOKING
PROPERLY EXPLAINED
WITH RECIPES

By the same author

Slow Cooking Properly Explained
Food Processors Properly Explained

Illustrations by Emma Thomas

Where to find *Right Way*

Elliot *Right Way* take pride in our editorial quality, accuracy and value-for-money. Booksellers everywhere can rapidly obtain any *Right Way* book for you. If you have been particularly pleased with any one title, do please mention this to your bookseller as personal recommendation helps us enormously.

Please send to the address on the back of the title page opposite, a stamped, self-addressed envelope if you would like a copy of our *free catalogue.* Alternatively, you may wish to browse through our extensive range of informative titles arranged by subject on the Internet at **www.right-way.co.uk**

We welcome views and suggestions from readers as well as from prospective authors; do please write to us or e-mail:
info@right-way.co.uk

PRESSURE COOKING PROPERLY EXPLAINED

WITH RECIPES

Dianne Page

RIGHT WAY

Typeset in 11/12 pt Times by Letterpart Ltd., Reigate, Surrey.

Printed and bound in Great Britain by Cox & Wyman Ltd., Reading, Berkshire.

The *Right Way* series is published by Elliot Right Way Books, Brighton Road, Lower Kingswood, Tadworth, Surrey, KT20 6TD, U.K. For information about our company and the other books we publish, visit our web site at www.right-way.co.uk

CONTENTS

CHAPTER   PAGE

Introduction   7
  Advantages of Pressure Cooking   8
  Pressure Cooking Explained in Brief   9
  Choosing a Pressure Cooker   10
  Using a Pressure Cooker   13
  Looking After Your Pressure Cooker   16
  Adapting Recipes for Pressure Cooking   17
  About the Recipes   18

1. Soups   19
2. Meat   43
3. Poultry and Game   65
4. Fish   81
5. Vegetables and Rice   93
6. Puddings   109
7. Cooking for One   132
8. Preserves   143

Index   157

INTRODUCTION

This book is particularly for newcomers to pressure cooking and for those of you whose pressure cooker is languishing unused at the back of a cupboard. It contains a wide variety of recipes that are sure to appeal and encourage you to try pressure cooking for yourself. Readers who are already fans of pressure cooking will find all their favourite recipes and plenty more.

Thankfully, the old wives' tales about exploding pressure cookers are a relic of the past. Today's cleverly designed models make sure to put your safety first.

My first pressure cooker was a wedding present. After preparing two or three meals, carefully following instructions, I soon found that pressure cooking is straightforward and gives excellent results, quickly and conveniently. It wasn't long before the pressure cooker became a way of life – just one more pan in the kitchen. The secret is to keep it handy, for there is no truer saying than 'out of sight, out of mind'. You too will find that pressure cooking can be an ideal, if not essential, part of a busy life. So discover for yourself how the speed of pressure cooking can extend a busy cook's repertoire to include homely everyday meals, as well as more adventurous menus.

Advantages of Pressure Cooking

Speedy
If you have never used a pressure cooker before, you will be
amazed at the short cooking times. Cooking under pressure
generally takes roughly one quarter to one third of the conventional cooking time. In some recipes the time saving is even
greater and can be quicker than in a microwave. For example,
a beef stew that normally takes about 1½ hours to cook
conventionally can be pressure cooked in 15–20 minutes.

The speed of pressure cooking means that those traditional
well-loved recipes, often neglected because they need hours
of cooking or close attention, can be prepared quickly and
easily. Old favourites like Steak and Kidney Pudding,
Steamed Suet Pudding and Lemon Curd are good examples.
Dried pulses (peas and beans) can be cooked in a fraction of
the normal time too.

Economical
The shorter cooking times inevitably result in fuel savings.
Remember too that, once the required cooking pressure has
been reached, the heat is usually turned down to minimum
setting for the remainder of the cooking time.

Even greater savings can be made if you cook more than
one kind of food in the pressure cooker at the same time – a
great advantage if you cook mainly for one or two or if you
are keen to economise. Turn to Chapter 7 for some suitable
menu ideas for one.

Pressure cooking can be economical when cooking for
crowds too, or when bulk cooking for the freezer. It is often
worthwhile cooking double the amount you need and freezing
half (the additional time taken to prepare extra ingredients is
negligible). Remember that increasing the quantity of ingredients (particularly in soups and stews) does not usually result
in a longer pressure cooking time. The time only needs
adjusting if you increase the size of foods such as meat joints
or steamed puddings. The main point to remember is never to
over-fill the pressure cooker.

Savings don't stop with fuel either. A pressure cooker will quickly cook cheaper cuts of meat – the ones that are packed with flavour but normally need long slow cooking to make them tender. Dried beans, usually a cheap source of protein, can be pressure cooked in just 20 minutes.

Improved Flavour, Colour and Nutrition
We all recognise the welcoming aroma of a delicious casserole bubbling away gently in the oven or on the hob, but it's easy to forget that, along with the steam, some of the flavour is also escaping. A pressure cooker is designed to seal in the steam and, as a result, retain most of the flavour.

Pressure cooking also helps to prevent the loss of colour that occurs in long, slow cooking – particularly in vegetables.

No matter how food is cooked, it's inevitable that a certain amount of nutritional value will be lost. Nevertheless, the short cooking times in a pressure cooker, combined with the small quantity of liquid and the absence of light and air, help to retain vitamins and minerals which might normally be lost.

Less Steam and Reduced Cooking Smells
A pressure cooker allows only a small amount of steam to escape, which enables you to cook steamed puddings and stews without the windows running with condensation. Cooking smells in the kitchen are reduced for the same reason.

A Boon for Camping, Caravanning and Boating
A pressure cooker is invaluable on self-catering holidays where time and space for cooking are at a premium.

Pressure Cooking Explained in Brief
When cooking in a saucepan, heat is lost as steam escapes from under the lid. A pressure cooker's lid fits so closely that an airtight seal is formed, trapping in the steam and allowing pressure to build up inside.

When water boils in a saucepan it is impossible for it to become hotter than boiling point (100°C). If water is heated under pressure, it *is* possible to increase that temperature and therefore cook the food more quickly.

Today's popular pressure cookers operate at three different pressures: Low (5 lb per square inch), Medium (10 lb per square inch) and High (15 lb per square inch) pressure. At Low pressure, water reaches 109°C; at Medium 115°C; and at High 121°C. Since most food is usually pressure cooked at High pressure, you can appreciate how that extra 21°C helps to speed up cooking significantly.

Choosing a Pressure Cooker

All pressure cookers work on the basic principle described above. How they usually differ is in the way they operate. Some pressure cookers have a choice of three different pressures (see above), some have two, while some older models have only one fixed pressure.

A pressure cooker with a choice of three pressures is very versatile and will cook a wide variety of food. For example, Low (5 lb) pressure is ideal for cooking a pudding that contains a raising agent (this ensures that the pudding rises before it 'sets') or for bottling fruit. Medium (10 lb) pressure is recommended for softening fruit for jam or jelly making. High (15 lb) pressure is ideal for everyday cooking of soups, vegetables and casserole-type dishes.

Pressure cookers that have two pressures usually cook at 6 lb and 12 lb. This means that cooking temperatures are a little lower and cooking times are slightly longer.

Pressure cookers with a single fixed pressure tend to operate at just 7½ lb. Again, this means that cooking temperatures are lower and cooking times are longer. At 7½ lb pressure, recipes that recommend High (15 lb) need twice the cooking time.

Before buying a pressure cooker, decide which size you need. Even the smaller models will cook a stew for four people but might not be large enough for a big joint of meat, bulk cooking for the freezer or for fruit bottling. On the one hand, pressure cookers can last 20 to 25 years, so it might be worth looking ahead and planning for the future when you buy. On the other hand, do not be tempted to choose the

A typical pressure cooker with weight. Some models offer a choice of three pressures while others have two.

largest pressure cooker you can find if you don't cook in large quantities on a regular basis. Remember too that you will need a convenient place to store it.

Assess the weight of the pressure cooker by lifting it and imagining it with the additional weight of the food. Make sure the pressure cooker has a thick base because, as you will see later in the book, it needs to withstand sudden drops in temperature when it is taken hot from the hob to stand in a bowl of cold water to reduce pressure. Without a sturdy base, in time, the bottom of the pressure cooker might bow, causing the pressure cooker to become inefficient.

In some models, a clockwork timer activates an automatic pressure-reducing device at the end of the chosen cooking time (you will need to remember to switch off the heat immediately, otherwise the cooker would eventually boil dry).

Accessories vary from model to model but basically every pressure cooker has a removable rack or trivet, which is used to hold food that is to be steam cooked above the water level

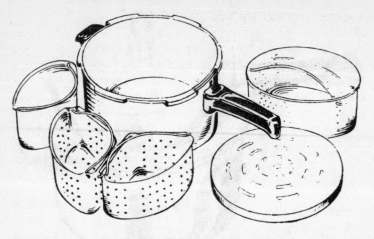

Typical pressure cooker accessories can include (from left to right): an unperforated basket, perforated baskets, trivet and blanching basket.

(necessary with vegetables, for example, particularly when more than one type is cooked at the same time). Baskets are often supplied and these are designed to keep foods separate so that their different flavours do not intermingle. The baskets are usually perforated to allow the steam to circulate. Sometimes, an unperforated basket is provided for cooking food such as egg custards, rice or stewed apple. Additional accessories might include separators or a basket for blanching vegetables for the freezer.

Finally, please have no fears about the safety of today's pressure cookers. Those made by reputable manufacturers have been perfected over the years and are utterly safe to use. They are fitted with several devices, each designed to release pressure in the unlikely event that a vent has become blocked or the pressure cooker has been allowed to boil dry and over-heat.

Make sure your model has a well-written instruction book from the manufacturer.

Using a Pressure Cooker

Before using a pressure cooker for the first time, read the manufacturer's instruction book carefully – it will tell you all you need to know about its operation (an obvious point, I know, but important nonetheless). In the meantime, here is a brief outline of how to use one.

A pressure cooker must contain a small amount of liquid in order to produce the steam to raise the pressure. The longer the cooking time, the more liquid is needed. Generally, the minimum recommended by manufacturers for cooking times up to 30 minutes is 300ml/½ pt. This liquid can be water, stock, beer, cider, wine, soup, or any combination of these. (Do not attempt to use oil as the cooking liquid – it's dangerous because it cannot create steam.) It is important to use the correct amount of liquid recommended for the recipe – too little could cause the pressure cooker to boil dry and overheat.

When cooking soups or casseroles, the trivet isn't needed as the flavours should intermingle during cooking. Some recipes require vegetables and meat to be softened or browned first and this can be done in the open base of the pressure cooker before adding the liquid and remaining ingredients. When you use the trivet, it is a good idea to put the water into the pressure cooker first – the water can't always be seen below the trivet and this way you avoid the risk of forgetting to add it.

After adding the ingredients to the pressure cooker, the lid is fitted carefully, making sure that it is locked tightly in position before allowing the pressure to rise. For pressure cookers with long, saucepan-type handles this means that the lid handle should lie directly over the base handle.

Once the lid is in position, the pressure cooker can be brought to pressure. The method depends on the type of pressure cooker.

1. Visual Pressure Indicator

The visual pressure indicator weight is a neat device which contains a plunger that rises and falls as the pressure rises and falls. It is marked with two or three rings and, as each ring appears, it shows which pressure has been reached.

A visual pressure indicator weight, in which a plunger rises and falls as the pressure inside the pressure cooker rises and falls.

When the lid has been fitted and the heat is turned on under the pressure cooker, the liquid inside it heats up. As it boils, it creates steam, which causes the pressure (and the plunger) to rise. As soon as the plunger shows the correct number of rings, the heat is turned down so that the plunger remains steady (without any hissing or spluttering) and pressure is maintained. If it does hiss and splutter, it means that the heat is too high. If you are already using minimum heat, you may need to move the pressure cooker gently half way off the ring (this is particularly relevant to electric hobs with solid and radiant plates). If the heat has been turned down too low, the pressure will drop and the plunger will fall slightly. Simply increase the heat a little until you have found the correct heat to maintain pressure.

2. Audible Pressure Indicator
This type indicates when pressure is reached by the noise it makes. The weight usually consists of three parts that are screwed together for cooking at three different pressures.

After fitting the lid, the weight is clicked on to the central vent, the heat is turned on, the liquid inside boils and the pressure rises. As this happens, the pressure cooker will start to hiss slightly. As soon as you hear a louder hissing sound this means that pressure has been reached and the heat should

An audible pressure indicator weight usually consists of three parts that are screwed together for cooking at different pressures.

be reduced until only a gentle mutter can be heard. As with the previous type of pressure weight, it may be necessary to draw the pressure cooker slightly off a solid or radiant electric ring to maintain the correct sound. If the pressure cooker becomes silent, it means that the pressure has dropped too far and the heat should be increased slightly.

3. Fixed Pressure Value
This type has a valve that rotates (or spins) when pressure is reached and usually operates at one pressure. Once the lid is in position, the valve is positioned on the air vent. The heat is turned on and, as the liquid inside boils, so pressure increases. As soon as the valve starts to spin, the heat should be reduced until it stops rotating.

No matter which type of pressure cooker you use, the cooking time is calculated from the moment pressure is reached – from the moment when the plunger shows the required ring, or when the pressure cooker starts to hiss loudly, or when the rotating valve starts to spin. How long it takes to reach pressure depends largely on what is inside the pressure cooker. If it contains only a few potatoes and carrots with 300ml/½ pt water, it won't take long. If, on the other hand, 1.2 litre/2 pt of stock is to be brought to the boil, it will take longer. It is important not to exceed the cooking times because delicate foods can easily overcook.

At the end of the cooking time, the pressure can be reduced in one of two ways.

To reduce the pressure quickly:
Stand the pressure cooker in a bowl of cold water.

Use this method for food which is likely to spoil if overcooked and for food that is cooked in only a small amount of liquid.

To reduce the pressure slowly at room temperature:
Turn off the heat, gently move the pressure cooker to a cold part of the hob (or stand it on a wooden chopping board or heat-resistant surface) and leave it to cool. Use this method for foods that are likely to froth up a lot during pressure cooking – such as soups, rice or dried beans and peas.

With the visual pressure indicator, the plunger drops down and the automatic air vent in the lid falls as the pressure reduces.

With the audible pressure indicator, wait until it is silent then, using a fork, tip the weight slightly and, if no steam escapes, lift it off.

With the fixed pressure valve, reduce pressure by lifting the rotating valve slightly to release the steam.

Remember that, for the food to cook there must be room for the steam to circulate. Do not fill the pressure cooker more than two thirds full of solid food such as vegetables. With recipes that contain a lot of liquid and are likely to froth up (such as soups, casseroles, milk puddings, rice and jam) the pressure cooker should not be filled more than half full.

Looking After Your Pressure Cooker
Each time you use your pressure cooker, check that the vent pipe and other safety devices are clean and free to operate.

After use, wash the pressure cooker parts in hot, soapy water, rinse and dry. Check your manufacturer's instruction book because some parts may not be suitable for immersing in water.

The rubber-like gasket may shrink slightly after a considerable time and so it is a good idea to stretch it (gently) occasionally while it is cold. If in time steam starts to escape from under the lid, it probably means that the gasket needs replacing. This, along with other spare parts, can be obtained direct from the manufacturer if you can't find them at a local shop.

Store the pressure cooker with its lid upside down on the base (you may like to put a cloth between them to prevent scratching). This way, there is no stress on the gasket and all the parts will be well ventilated. If the weight is separate from the lid, make sure it is kept somewhere safe where it can't be damaged.

Adapting Recipes for Pressure Cooking
The easiest way is to refer to similar recipes in this book, or in the manufacturer's instruction book, and follow the same method. If in doubt, work out which ingredient needs the longest cooking time and use that as your guide.

When the quantity of food is increased, it is only necessary to extend the cooking time if you are cooking a larger joint of meat or steamed pudding, in which case the heat has to penetrate a greater bulk.

The cooking time governs how much liquid is needed and manufacturers give instructions in their books. Remember that when pressure cooking stews and casseroles, there won't be as much evaporation as with conventional cooking, so you won't need quite so much liquid. All the same, don't forget to include at least the minimum amount of liquid recommended by the manufacturer.

Stews and meat dishes can be thickened slightly before cooking but use no more than 25g/1 oz flour, otherwise the steam may find it difficult to circulate adequately and the food may burn on the bottom. Stir the thickened dish well before pressure cooking to prevent food sticking. If further thickening is required, this should be done after cooking.

About the Recipes

The recipes in this book were tested using the following pressures:

High	15 lb
Medium	10 lb
Low	5 lb

If your pressure cooker operates at pressures different from these, here are some tips:

- Check with a similar recipe in your manufacturer's instruction/recipe book and use the cooking time as a guide.
- When a recipe in this book cooks at High pressure and you need to use a lower pressure (say 12 lb), add one quarter to one third of the recommended cooking time, using the ingredient with the longest cooking time as a guide.
- When a recipe cooks at High pressure and you need to use a lower pressure (say 7½ lb), double the cooking time, using the ingredient with the longest cooking time as a guide.
- When a recipe cooks at Medium and you need to use a higher pressure (say 12 lb), reduce the cooking time by a few minutes, using the ingredient with the longest cooking time as a guide.
- When a recipe cooks at Low and you need to use a higher pressure (say 6 lb or 7½ lb), reduce the cooking time slightly, using the ingredient with the longest cooking time as a guide.

1

SOUPS

Soup making, like bread making and growing your own vegetables, has become very popular over the years. Why do people bother? If you've tasted bread fresh from the oven and beans fresh from the garden you will understand why people take the trouble to make their own soup. But is it trouble? Certainly not with a pressure cooker.

When making soup in a saucepan, the preparation and finishing off are often the shortest parts of the whole process. It's the long simmering that takes the time and ties you to the kitchen. With a pressure cooker, soups can be ready in minutes.

Once you have tried home-made soup you will be reluctant to use tins or packets again. Furthermore, you will become

Scrooge-like about leftovers and vegetable peelings. Well washed peelings make an ideal base for a soup so don't waste their goodness.

When a recipe calls for stock, don't automatically turn to a stock cube. With your pressure cooker you can prepare real stock in 30 to 40 minutes. Apart from a rather smug feeling of cooking 'properly', there is no doubt that the flavour is much better, especially for more delicately flavoured dishes.

When experimenting with your own favourite soup recipes, I suggest you follow these guidelines for best results.

The trivet is not needed when making soup or stock as the idea is to mingle all the flavours together in the liquid.

Don't fill your pressure cooker more than half full of liquid as it needs room to boil up when cooking. When cooking soup for a large number, make sure that the liquid level doesn't exceed the half-way mark – you can always add the rest of the liquid at the end of the cooking time and bring the soup to the boil again in the open pressure cooker.

When reducing pressure, do this slowly at room temperature. Simply switch off the heat and gently move the pressure cooker to a cool part of the hob.

When converting your own recipes, remember there is less evaporation with pressure cooking. This means that you don't have to allow for the extra liquid which normally boils away. Always remember, though, to ensure that you have in your pressure cooker at least the minimum amount of liquid recommended by your manufacturer's instructions – usually 300ml/½ pt.

Season in moderation before pressure cooking the soup. It is always preferable to add more salt and pepper at the end rather than try to correct an over-salty soup.

Always add the thickening at the end of the cooking.

When making a basic stock, more flavour is obtained from bones if they are cut small, so ask your butcher to chop them for you. Some ingredients are not suitable for stock making, including green vegetables, milk, gravy, thickened sauces, bread and potatoes.

When preparing soup in quantity for the freezer, remember the earlier point about not filling the pressure cooker above the half-way mark (see above). Then, instead of adding the extra liquid at the end of the cooking, it is a good idea to freeze the soup in its concentrated form as it takes up less space. Add the remaining liquid when thawing and re-heating.

When calculating the cooking time for your own soup recipes, compare the ingredients with those of the following recipes. The ingredient that takes the longest to cook will dictate the cooking time.

STOCK

Makes about 600ml/1 pt   *40 minutes at High pressure*

This stock will be more or less concentrated, depending on the quantity of bones used. As with soups generally, it is easier to dilute after cooking rather than make too weak a stock to start with. If you do not intend to use it within 3–4 days, it is best frozen.

Bones or poultry carcass (cooked or raw)
2 carrots, scrubbed and sliced
1 onion, roughly chopped
6 peppercorns
Bouquet garni
1 tsp salt

1. Put the bones or carcass into the pressure cooker and pour over 1 litre/1¾ pt water. Bring slowly to the boil in the open pan and, with a spoon, remove the scum from the surface with a spoon.

2. Add the remaining ingredients.

3. Fit the lid, bring to High pressure and cook for 40 minutes.

4. Reduce the pressure slowly at room temperature.

5. Cool slightly, strain into a container and, when cold, remove the fat from the top.

6. Chill until needed – up to 3–4 days.

LETTUCE SOUP

Serves 4   *7 minutes at High pressure*

This soup freezes well and is a great way to use up surplus lettuce from the garden.

25g/1 oz butter
1 onion, finely chopped
1 large potato, chopped
1 lettuce, roughly chopped
600ml/1 pt chicken stock
600ml/1 pt milk
Salt and freshly ground black pepper
Single cream, to serve
Chopped fresh parsley, to serve

1. Melt the butter in the open pressure cooker and gently cook the onion, stirring occasionally, until softened but not browned.

2. Add the potato, lettuce, stock, milk and seasoning. Bring to the boil in the open pan, then lower the heat to a simmer.

3. Fit the lid, bring to High pressure and cook for 7 minutes.

4. Reduce the pressure slowly at room temperature. Cool slightly and process, liquidize or sieve the soup to a purée. Adjust the seasoning to taste.

5. To serve hot, return the soup to the open pressure cooker and reheat. To serve cold, chill in the refrigerator after it has cooled.

6. Swirl a little cream into each serving and scatter over some chopped parsley.

WATERCRESS SOUP

Serves 4–6   *7 minutes at High pressure*

Make a meal out of this filling soup by serving it with fresh crusty bread.

1 bunch of watercress, washed and roughly chopped
25g/1 oz butter
1 onion, finely chopped
450g/1 lb main-crop potatoes, peeled and diced
1 litre/1¾ pt chicken or vegetable stock
Salt and freshly ground black pepper
4 tbsp crème fraîche or soured cream

1. Reserve a few watercress leaves for serving.

2. Melt the butter in the open pressure cooker and gently cook the onion and potatoes, stirring occasionally, until softened but not browned.

3. Add the watercress, stock and seasoning.

4. Fit the lid, bring to High pressure and cook for 7 minutes.

5. Reduce the pressure slowly at room temperature. Cool slightly and process, liquidize or sieve the soup to a purée.

6. Return the soup to the open pressure cooker and bring just to the boil, adjusting the seasoning to taste.

7. Top each serving with a spoonful of crème fraîche or soured cream and the reserved watercress leaves.

CELERY SOUP

Serves 4   *10 minutes at High pressure*

For the best flavour and colour, use the whole head of celery – stalks and leaves. Try serving the soup topped with tiny pieces of crisp-grilled bacon – delicious!

1 head of celery, chopped
25g/1 oz butter
1 onion, chopped
850ml/1½ pt chicken or vegetable stock
Salt and freshly ground black pepper
25g/1 oz cornflour
300ml/½ pt milk

1. Reserve a few of the smallest celery leaves for serving.

2. Melt the butter in the open pressure cooker and gently cook the celery and onion, stirring occasionally, until softened but not browned.

3. Stir in the stock and add seasoning.

4. Fit the lid, bring to High pressure and cook for 10 minutes.

5. Reduce the pressure slowly at room temperature. Cool slightly and process, liquidize or sieve the soup to a purée.

6. Return the soup to the open pressure cooker. Blend the cornflour with the milk to make a smooth mixture and stir in. Heat, stirring, until the soup comes to the boil and has thickened slightly.

7. Adjust the seasoning to taste and serve topped with the reserved celery leaves.

FRESH TOMATO SOUP

Serves 4   *4 minutes at High pressure*

I use the tomatoes whole, skins and all. If you prefer, remove the skins by pouring over sufficient boiling water to cover the tomatoes. After a minute or two, they should slip off easily.

2 streaky bacon rashers, finely chopped
1 onion, finely chopped
675g/1½ lb ripe tomatoes, quartered
600ml/1 pt chicken or vegetable stock
1 tsp sugar
Salt and freshly ground black pepper
Worcestershire sauce
1 tbsp cornflour
Chopped fresh parsley, to serve

1. In the open pressure cooker, gently cook the bacon until the fat begins to run. Add the onion and cook gently, stirring occasionally, until softened but not browned.

2. Add the tomatoes, stock, sugar, seasoning and a dash of Worcestershire sauce.

3. Fit the lid, bring to High pressure and cook for 4 minutes.

4. Reduce the pressure slowly at room temperature. Cool slightly and process, liquidize or sieve the soup to a purée.

5. Return the soup to the open pressure cooker. Blend the cornflour with 150ml/¼ pt water to make a smooth mixture and stir in. Heat, stirring, until the soup comes to the boil and has thickened slightly.

6. Season to taste and sprinkle with chopped parsley.

VICHYSSOISE

Traditionally this soup is served chilled. In my opinion, it is equally good served hot.

Serves 4–6   *5 minutes at High pressure*

25g/1 oz butter
White parts only of 3 large leeks, sliced
1 onion, chopped
450g/1 lb main-crop potatoes, chopped
850ml/1½ pt chicken or vegetable stock
Salt and freshly ground pepper
300ml/½ pt single cream
Snipped chives, to garnish

1. Melt the butter in the open pressure cooker and gently cook the leeks and onion, stirring occasionally, until softened but not browned.

2. Add the potatoes, stock and seasoning.

3. Fit the lid, bring to High pressure and cook for 5 minutes.

4. Reduce the pressure slowly at room temperature. Cool slightly and process, liquidize or sieve the soup to a purée. Adjust the seasoning to taste.

5. Chill in the refrigerator and, just before serving, stir in the cream and garnish with chives. If serving hot, stir in the cream and reheat gently without boiling.

BROAD BEAN AND BACON SOUP

Serves 4   *5 minutes at High pressure*

Broad beans and bacon complement each other wonderfully.
Feel free to use fresh or frozen beans.

115g/4 oz streaky bacon, finely chopped
1 onion, chopped
450g/1 lb broad beans (weighed after shelling)
850ml/1½ pt chicken stock
300ml/½ pt milk
Salt and freshly ground black pepper
Snipped chives, to garnish

1. In the open pressure cooker, gently cook the bacon until
    the fat begins to run. Add the onion and cook gently,
    stirring occasionally, until softened but not browned.

2. Add the broad beans, stock, milk and seasoning. Bring
    to the boil in the open pan, then lower the heat to a
    simmer.

3. Fit the lid, bring to High pressure and cook for 5
    minutes.

4. Reduce the pressure slowly at room temperature. Cool
    slightly and process, liquidize or sieve the soup to a
    purée.

5. Return the soup to the open pressure cooker and adjust
    the seasoning to taste. Reheat and serve garnished with
    chives.

MINESTRONE

Serves 4–6   *8 minutes at High pressure*

The ingredients for this soup can be varied, depending on what is in season, but as you can see the ideal Minestrone contains a large variety of vegetables.

2 streaky bacon rashers, finely chopped
1 tbsp olive oil
1 onion, finely chopped
1 garlic clove, crushed
3 medium carrots, cut into small dice
¼ cabbage, finely shredded
4 celery sticks, thinly sliced
25g/1 oz peas (fresh or frozen)
1 tbsp tomato purée
Salt and freshly ground black pepper
1 litre/1¾ pt chicken stock
55g/2 oz macaroni or broken pieces of spaghetti
Freshly grated Parmesan cheese

1. In the open pressure cooker, gently cook the bacon until the fat begins to run. Add the oil and the vegetables and cook gently for 5–10 minutes, stirring occasionally, until softened but not browned.

2. Add the tomato purée, seasoning, stock and pasta.

3. Fit the lid, bring to High pressure and cook for 8 minutes.

4. Reduce the pressure slowly at room temperature.

5. Adjust the seasoning and serve sprinkled with Parmesan cheese.

MIXED VEGETABLE SOUP

Serves 4-6   *10 minutes at High pressure*

Served with crusty bread, this could be a main course soup.
Vary your choice of vegetables according to the seasons.

25g/1 oz butter
2 medium onions, finely chopped
4 large carrots, cut into 1cm/½ in slices
2 large parsnips, cut into 1cm/½ in slices
4 large potatoes, cut into 1cm/½ in slices
2 medium leeks, thinly sliced
1 litre/1¾ pt chicken, beef or vegetable stock
Salt and freshly ground black pepper
Dash of Worcestershire sauce
Freshly grated Cheddar cheese, to serve (optional)

1. Melt the butter in the open pressure cooker and gently
    cook the onions, stirring occasionally, until softened but
    not browned.

2. Add the remaining ingredients.

3. Fit the lid, bring to High pressure and cook for 10
    minutes.

4. Reduce the pressure slowly at room temperature. Adjust
    the seasoning to taste and serve just as it is or topped
    with grated cheese.

FRENCH ONION SOUP

Serves 4   *4 minutes at High pressure*

I like to float the cheese-topped bread on the surface of the soup. You may prefer to put it in the bottom of the serving bowl before ladling the soup over the top.

25g/1 oz butter
1 tbsp olive oil
450g/1 lb onions, thinly sliced
1 litre/1¾ pt beef stock
Salt and freshly ground black pepper
Freshly grated cheese, such as Gruyère or Cheddar
4 thick slices of French bread

1. Heat the butter and oil in the open pressure cooker and gently cook the onions for 10–15 minutes, stirring occasionally, or until golden brown.

2. Add the stock and seasoning.

3. Fit the lid, bring to High pressure and cook for 4 minutes.

4. Reduce the pressure slowly at room temperature.

5. Adjust the seasoning to taste.

6. Pile the cheese on the bread and toast under the grill until the cheese bubbles and begins to brown.

7. Float a slice of bread, cheese side uppermost, on each bowl of soup.

CARROT AND ORANGE SOUP

Serves 4–6   *5 minutes at High pressure*

This is a refreshingly light soup that's ideal for serving as a starter.

25g/1 oz butter
1 onion, finely chopped
675g/1½ lb carrots, thinly sliced
850ml/1½ pt chicken or vegetable stock
Finely grated rind and juice of 2 oranges
Salt and freshly ground black pepper
1 tsp sugar
Chopped fresh parsley, to garnish

1. Melt the butter in the open pressure cooker and gently cook the onion, stirring occasionally, until softened but not browned.

2. Add the carrots, stock, grated orange rind, seasoning and sugar.

3. Fit the lid, bring to High pressure and cook for 5 minutes.

4. Reduce the pressure slowly at room temperature.

5. Stir in the orange juice, cool slightly and process, liquidize or sieve the soup to a purée.

6. Return the soup to the open pressure cooker and adjust the seasoning to taste. Reheat and serve sprinkled with parsley.

LENTIL SOUP

Serves 4   *10 minutes at High pressure*

There's no need to soak the lentils before making this soup.
Make it with red or green lentils. It's delicious served with
bits of crisp-fried bacon scattered over the top. A hunk of
crusty bread makes it into a meal.

25g/1 oz butter
1 onion, chopped
115g/4 oz lentils
1 litre/1¾ pt chicken stock
2 tbsp tomato purée
Salt and freshly ground black pepper
Bay leaf (optional)

1. Melt the butter in the open pressure cooker and gently
    cook the onion, stirring occasionally, until golden
    brown.

2. Stir in the remaining ingredients.

3. Fit the lid, bring to High pressure and cook for 10
    minutes.

4. Reduce the pressure slowly at room temperature.
    Remove and discard the bay leaf, if used. Cool slightly
    then process, liquidize or sieve the soup to a purée.

5. Return the soup to the open pressure cooker and adjust
    the seasoning to taste. Reheat and serve.

SPLIT PEA AND BACON SOUP

Serves 4–6   *15 minutes at High pressure*

No need to soak the peas overnight – simply cover them with boiling water and leave to stand for 1 hour.

4 streaky bacon rashers, finely chopped
1 large onion, chopped
175g/6 oz dried split peas, soaked and drained as above
1 litre/1¾ pt chicken or vegetable stock
Sprig of fresh mint
Salt and freshly ground black pepper
Crème fraîche or thick Greek yoghurt, to serve
Finely chopped fresh mint, to serve

1. In the open pressure cooker, gently cook the bacon until the fat begins to run. Add the onion and cook gently, stirring occasionally, until golden brown.

2. Add the peas, stock, mint and seasoning. Bring to the boil, then lower the heat to a simmer.

3. Fit the lid, bring to High pressure and cook for 15 minutes.

4. Reduce the pressure slowly at room temperature.

5. Remove and discard the mint. Cool slightly and process, liquidize or sieve the soup to a purée.

6. Return the soup to the open pressure cooker, adjust the seasoning to taste and reheat.

7. On to each serving, drop a spoonful of crème fraîche or yoghurt and a little chopped fresh mint.

FISH STOCK

15 minutes at High pressure

There's nothing quite like the delicate flavour of a home-made fish stock. Chill and use it the same day or freeze it for future use.

1 fish head and trimmings
1 onion, chopped
1 celery stick, sliced
6 peppercorns
A few parsley sprigs
Bouquet garni
1 tsp salt

1. Wash the fish head and trimmings and put into the pressure cooker with the remaining ingredients. Pour over 1 litre/1¾ pt water.

2. Fit the lid, bring to High pressure and cook for 15 minutes.

3. Reduce the pressure slowly at room temperature.

4. Strain the stock. It's now ready to use.

MEDITERRANEAN FISH SOUP

Serves 4   *5 minutes at High pressure*

For the most delicious result, use at least two different types of fish. You could use any trimmings (skin and bones) to make your own fish stock (see page 35). Use a potato peeler to pare the strip of peel from a lemon.

**675g/1½ lb fish such as whiting, plaice, cod or haddock
  (weighed after removing skin and bones)
1 tbsp olive oil
1 onion, sliced
1 garlic clove, crushed
1 medium carrot, thinly sliced
200g can chopped tomatoes
850ml/1½ pt fish stock
150ml/¼ pt dry white wine
1 wide strip of lemon peel
Salt and freshly ground pepper
Chopped fresh parsley, to garnish**

1. Cut the fish into 5cm/2 in chunks.

2. Heat the oil in the open pressure cooker and gently cook the onion, stirring occasionally, until softened but not browned.

3. Add the garlic and the carrot and cook gently for 1–2 minutes.

4. Stir in the fish, tomatoes, stock, wine, lemon peel and seasoning.

5. Fit the lid, bring to High pressure and cook for 5 minutes.

6. Reduce the pressure slowly at room temperature.

7. Remove and discard the lemon peel, adjust the seasoning to taste and serve sprinkled with parsley.

SCOTCH BROTH

Serves 4   *20 minutes at High pressure*

To make this into a main-course soup, use double the amount of lamb – it will cook in the same time.

225g/8 oz middle neck of lamb, weighed after trimming off excess fat
1 litre/1¾ pt lamb stock or water
55g/2 oz pearl barley
1 large onion, finely chopped
1 carrot, cut into small dice
1 celery stalk, thinly sliced
1 small swede, cut into small dice
Salt and freshly ground black pepper

1. Cut from the bones as much lamb as you can and cut it into small pieces.

2. Put the lamb and bones into the open pressure cooker and add the stock or water. Bring to the boil and, with a spoon, remove any scum from the surface.

3. Stir in the remaining ingredients.

4. Fit the lid, bring to High pressure and cook for 20 minutes.

5. Reduce the pressure slowly at room temperature.

6. Remove the bones, scraping off any remaining meat.

7. Stir this meat into the soup, adjust the seasoning to taste and serve.

MULLIGATAWNY SOUP

Serves 4   *5 minutes at High pressure*

Make this soup as 'hot' as you like, depending on the type and quantity of curry powder you use. It's delicious accompanied with warm naan bread.

25g/1 oz butter
1 medium onion, chopped
1 medium carrot, cut into small dice
1 tbsp curry powder, or to taste
1 litre/1¾ pt beef stock
1 tbsp tomato purée
1 tbsp mango chutney
2 tsp cornflour
Chopped fresh coriander, to serve

1.   Melt the butter in the open pressure cooker and gently cook the onion and carrot, stirring occasionally, until softened but not browned.

2.   Stir in the curry powder and continue to cook over a gentle heat, stirring, for 2–3 minutes.

3.   Gradually stir in the stock, tomato purée and chutney.

4.   Fit the lid, bring to High pressure and cook for 5 minutes.

5.   Reduce the pressure slowly at room temperature. Cool slightly and process, liquidize or sieve the soup to a purée.

6.   Return the soup to the open pressure cooker. Blend the cornflour with a little cold water to make a thin paste and stir in. Bring to the boil, stirring continuously, until slightly thickened.

7.   Adjust the seasoning to taste and serve sprinkled with coriander.

COCK-A-LEEKIE

Serves 4   *7 minutes at High pressure*

This soup, based on the traditional Scottish version, takes only minutes in the pressure cooker.

4 skinless chicken thighs
1 litre/1¾ pt chicken stock
1 medium onion, finely chopped
4 medium leeks, cut into 2.5cm/1 in slices
4 ready-to-eat prunes, stones removed
Salt and freshly ground black pepper
1 tbsp lemon juice

1. Put the chicken into the pressure cooker with the stock. Bring to the boil and, with a spoon, skim the surface.

2. Stir in the remaining ingredients.

3. Fit the lid, bring to High pressure and cook for 7 minutes.

4. Reduce the pressure slowly at room temperature.

5. Lift out the chicken, cut the meat off the bones and chop into small pieces. Discard the bones.

6. Return the chopped chicken to the soup, adjust the seasoning to taste and reheat before serving.

CHICKEN SOUP WITH HERB DUMPLINGS

Serves 6   *10 minutes per 450g/1 lb at High pressure plus 15 minutes steaming*

This is substantial enough to serve as a main course.

Soup:
1 small chicken
1 litre/1¾ pt chicken stock or water
1 large onion, thinly sliced
2 medium carrots, thinly sliced
2 sticks celery, thinly sliced
Bay leaf
Salt and freshly ground black pepper

Dumplings:
85g/3 oz self-raising flour
25g/1 oz shredded suet
Pinch of salt
Freshly ground black pepper
1 tsp dried mixed herbs
Milk to mix

1. Weigh the chicken and put into the pressure cooker with the stock or water. Bring to the boil, then reduce the heat to a simmer. With a spoon, remove any scum from the surface. Stir in the remaining soup ingredients.

2. Fit the lid, bring to High pressure and cook for 10 minutes per 450g/1 lb.

3. Meanwhile, make the dumplings. Sieve the flour into a bowl and mix in the suet, seasoning and herbs. Stir in enough milk to make a soft dough. Divide the mixture into twelve equal portions and, with lightly floured hands, shape them into balls.

4.   Reduce the pressure slowly at room temperature.

5.   Lift out the chicken, remove the meat from the bones and cut it into small pieces. Return the chicken to the pressure cooker. Adjust the seasoning to taste.

6.   Bring the soup to the boil in the open pressure cooker and arrange the dumplings on top. Fit the lid *without the weight and without bringing to pressure*, lower the heat until only a thin stream of steam escapes and steam for 15 minutes.

CHICKEN AND MUSHROOM SOUP

Serves 4   *5 minutes at High pressure*

This soup is best made with fresh or home-made chicken stock so as not to overwhelm the delicate flavour of the mushrooms. I like to use basmati rice for its delicate, perfumed flavour.

1 litre/1¾ pt chicken stock
1 heaped tbsp long grain rice
Salt and freshly ground black pepper
115g/4 oz button mushrooms, sliced
Snipped chives, to garnish

1. Put the stock, rice, seasoning and mushrooms into the pressure cooker.

2. Fit the lid, bring to High pressure and cook for 5 minutes.

3. Reduce the pressure slowly at room temperature.

4. Adjust the seasoning to taste and serve, sprinkled with chives.

2

MEAT

A pressure cooker is a boon for cooking meat. Not only is the cooking time less than with conventional methods, but the super-heated steam penetrates the meat to make it really tender. Very little steam escapes during pressure cooking, so all the flavour is trapped inside.

Pressure cooking is a moist cooking method, which means that it's great for boiling, braising, casseroling, stewing and pot roasting.

Here are some guidelines for adapting your own meat recipes to pressure cooking:

The trivet: This is not used when cooking stews or casseroles.

Pressure: Use High pressure and, in general, reduce pressure quickly after cooking (unless the recipe uses a large quantity of liquid or recommends otherwise).

Quantity: Quantities can be increased but make sure the pressure cooker is no more than two thirds full.

Time: This is influenced very much by the quality of the meat, its size and thickness. You will soon get a 'feel' for timing but use these recipes and those in your instruction book as a guide. When increasing quantities for stews or casseroles, there is no need to increase the cooking time.

Thickening: Meat may be tossed in a tablespoon of seasoned flour before cooking to give a slightly thickened gravy, but if really thick stews are preferred, add extra thickening *after* pressure cooking, using flour or cornflour blended to a smooth paste with a little liquid. Too much thickening before cooking would restrict the amount of steam available for circulation, with the risk that food could stick to the base.

Liquid: Remember that there is less evaporation compared with oven or hob cooking. Consequently your adapted recipes won't need more than the recommended minimum of liquid. As a general rule, this is 300ml/½ pt for the first 20 minutes and 150ml/¼ pt for each extra 15 minutes cooking (check with your instruction book too).

Pot roasting: When choosing a joint of meat for pot roasting, make sure that it will fit inside your pressure cooker without blocking any of the air vents. Joints over 1.35kg (3 lb) are not really suitable for pressure cooking as the outside will over-cook before the centre is done. Follow the general method for Pot Roast, given on page 53, and use the following table as a guide to times and liquid.

Liquid and Cooking Times at High pressure			
	450g/1 lb	**900g/2 lb**	**1.35kg/3 lb**
Beef, lamb, mutton, pork, veal	300ml/½ pt 15 minutes	425ml/¾ pt 30 minutes	600ml/1 pt 45 minutes
Bacon, ham	300ml/½ pt 12 minutes	300ml/½ pt 24 minutes	425ml/¾ pt 36 minutes

Freezing

When cooking in bulk for the freezer, bear in mind the
following points:

Garlic reduces the storage time to 1 month, so if you plan
to freeze the food for longer, simply omit the garlic.

Do not thicken before freezing. It is best done after
reheating, using cornflour blended to a smooth paste with a
little liquid.

Freeze in single or double portions for convenience.

If food is to be reheated from frozen in the pressure cooker,
freeze it in shallow containers of a size that will fit inside the
pressure cooker. This helps reduce the reheating time, which
would be much greater were the food frozen in one large
square block.

To reheat, put 150ml/¼ pt water in the pressure cooker,
without the trivet. Remove the portions from their containers
and place in the water. Fit the lid and bring to pressure. The
reheating time will depend on the size of the portion but, as a
general rule, cook for 20 minutes at High pressure. Reduce
the pressure slowly at room temperature. If wished, thicken
before serving. If foil containers are used to contain the
frozen food, these may be stood on the trivet over 300ml½ pt
water and pressure cooked for 20 minutes at High pressure.

BEEF WITH VEGETABLES

Serves 4   *15 minutes at High pressure*

Use this recipe as the basis for a delicious stew, varying the meat and vegetables according to personal preference and seasonal availability.

675g/1½ lb lean stewing steak, cut into cubes
25g/1 oz flour
2 tbsp oil
2 medium onions, chopped
225g/8 oz carrots, sliced
450g/1 lb potatoes, thickly sliced
2 medium parsnips, sliced
2 medium leeks, sliced
600ml/1 pt beef or vegetable stock
Salt and freshly ground black pepper
1 bay leaf
1 tbsp parsley, chopped for garnish

1. Toss the steak in the flour (this is easy to do in a freezer bag).

2. Heat the oil in the open pressure cooker, add the onions and cook, stirring occasionally, until softened but not browned.

3. Add the steak and cook, stirring occasionally, until browned.

4. Add the remaining ingredients except the parsley. Fit the lid, bring to High pressure and cook for 15 minutes. Reduce the pressure quickly in cold water.

5. Remove the bay leaf, adjust the seasoning to taste and serve garnished with parsley.

BEEF GOULASH

Serves 4   *15 minutes at High pressure*

Based on one of Hungary's best-known dishes, this version is
a rich stew rather than a soup.

675g/1½ lb lean stewing steak, cut into cubes
25g/1 oz flour
2 tbsp oil
2 medium onions, chopped
3 tbsp paprika pepper
300ml/½ pt beef stock
2 tbsp tomato purée
1 tbsp dried mixed herbs
1 bay leaf
1 tsp salt

1.   Toss the steak in the flour (this is easy to do in a freezer
     bag).

2.   Heat the oil in the open pressure cooker, add the onions
     and cook, stirring occasionally, until softened and
     golden brown.

3.   Add the steak and cook, stirring occasionally, until
     browned.

4.   Add the paprika pepper and cook on a low heat, stirring,
     for 1 minute. Add the stock, tomato purée, herbs, bay
     leaf and salt.

5.   Fit the lid, bring to High pressure and cook for 15
     minutes.

6.   Reduce the pressure quickly in cold water.

7.   Remove the bay leaf before serving and adjust the
     seasoning to taste.

CURRIED BEEF

Serves 4   *15 minutes at High pressure*

Serve this with freshly cooked basmati rice, poppadums and chutneys.

675g/1½ lb lean stewing steak, cut into cubes
25g/1 oz flour
2 tbsp oil
1 medium onion, finely chopped
1 garlic clove, crushed
1 celery stalk, sliced
1 tbsp curry powder
300ml/½ pt beef stock
1 large eating apple, peeled, cored and chopped
1 tbsp lemon juice
1 heaped tbsp chutney, such as mango
25g/1 oz sultanas
Salt

1. Toss the steak in the flour (this is easy to do in a freezer bag).

2. Heat the oil in the open pressure cooker, add the onion, garlic and celery and cook, stirring occasionally, until softened but not browned.

3. Add the steak and cook, stirring occasionally, until browned.

4. Add the curry powder and cook on a low heat, stirring, for 1 minute.

5. Stir in the remaining ingredients.

6. Fit the lid, bring to High pressure and cook for 15 minutes.

7. Reduce the pressure quickly in cold water.

8. Adjust the seasoning to taste before serving.

BEEF IN BROWN ALE

Serves 4   *15 minutes at High pressure*

Buttered tagliatelle makes a great accompaniment here. You could make this into Beef Carbonnade by topping the cooked dish with some French bread slices, toasted on the upper side and spread with extra French mustard on the underside.

675g/1½ lb lean stewing steak, cut into cubes
25g/1 oz flour
25g/1 oz butter
2 lean streaky bacon rashers, chopped
2 medium onions, chopped
300ml/½ pt brown ale
150ml/¼ pt beef stock
1 tbsp French mustard
2 tsp sugar
Salt and freshly ground black pepper
Bouquet garni

1. Toss the steak in the flour (this is easy to do in a freezer bag).

2. Melt the butter in the open pressure cooker, add the bacon and onions and cook, stirring occasionally, until softened but not browned.

3. Add the steak and cook, stirring occasionally, until browned.

4. Add the beer, stock, mustard, sugar, seasoning and bouquet garni.

5. Fit the lid, bring to High pressure and cook for 15 minutes. Reduce the pressure quickly in cold water.

6. Remove the bouquet garni and adjust the seasoning to taste before serving.

STEAK AND KIDNEY PUDDING

Serves 4–6   *Filling: 15 minutes at High pressure*
                      Pudding: 20 minutes steaming, then
                      30 minutes at Low pressure

This great old-fashioned savoury pudding is perfect for pressure cooking. It takes less than half the conventional (steaming) time.

Filling:
675g/1½ lb lean stewing steak, cut into cubes
115g/4 oz lamb or ox kidney, sliced
25g/1 oz flour
2 tbsp oil
1 medium onion, chopped
225g/8 oz mushrooms, thickly sliced if large
Salt and freshly ground black pepper
300ml/½ pt beef stock or Guinness

Suet pastry:
225g/8 oz self-raising flour
½ tsp salt
115g/4 oz shredded suet

1. Toss the steak and kidney in the flour (this is easy to do in a freezer bag).

2. Heat the oil in the open pressure cooker, add the onion and cook, stirring occasionally, until softened but not browned.

3. Add the steak mixture and cook, stirring occasionally, until browned.

4. Stir in the mushrooms, seasoning and stock or Guinness.

5. Fit the lid, bring to High pressure and cook for 15 minutes.

6. Reduce the pressure quickly in cold water. Turn into a container and leave to cool while preparing the pastry.

7. Sift the flour and salt into a mixing bowl and stir in the suet. With a flat-blade knife, gradually stir in about 150ml/¼ pt cold water, using sufficient to make a soft, scone-like dough.

8. Reserve one third of the dough for the lid and roll the remaining dough into a circle, large enough to line a 1 litre/1¾ pt pudding basin. Grease the basin and line it with the pastry.

9. Using a slotted spoon, fill the basin with the steak mixture to within 2.5cm/1" of the top, adding 3 tbsp of the gravy (reserve the remainder for serving separately).

10. Roll out the reserved pastry to make a lid, moisten the edges and crimp firmly into position, leaving a space up to the rim of the basin to allow the pastry to rise.

11. Cover securely with a double layer of greased grease-proof paper or a single layer of foil. Put the trivet and 1 litre/1¾ pt water into the cleaned pressure cooker. Stand the basin on the trivet.

12. Fit the lid *without the weight and without bringing to pressure* and steam for 20 minutes on a gentle heat.

13. Fit the lid, bring to Low pressure and cook for 30 minutes.

14. Reduce the pressure slowly at room temperature.

15. Serve the pudding with the reheated gravy.

Freezer note: The cooked pudding can be frozen. To defrost and reheat it, cook for 40 minutes at Low pressure using 1 litre/1¾ pt water.

BOLOGNESE SAUCE

Serves 4   *10 minutes at High pressure*

A classic sauce to serve with spaghetti, this is one of my
favourite recipes for bulk cooking – it is so useful as the basis
for many other dishes, like lasagne, stuffed peppers or cottage
pie.

2 tbsp olive oil
2 streaky bacon rashers, chopped
1 medium onion, chopped
1 garlic clove, crushed
2 celery stalks, thinly sliced
675g/1½ lb lean minced beef
400g can chopped tomatoes
150ml/¼ pt beef or vegetable stock
1 tsp Worcestershire sauce
Salt and freshly ground black pepper
1 tsp dried oregano
Bay leaf

1. Heat the oil in the open pressure cooker, add the bacon,
    onion, garlic and celery and cook, stirring occasionally,
    until softened but not browned.

2. Add the beef and cook, stirring occasionally until
    browned.

3. Stir in the remaining ingredients.

4. Fit the lid, bring to High pressure and cook for 10
    minutes.

5. Reduce the pressure quickly in cold water.

6. Remove the bay leaf and adjust the seasoning to taste-
    before serving.

BEEF POT ROAST

Serves 4–6   *30 minutes at High pressure*

Relish the mellow flavours that normally develop with long
slow cooking – in just half an hour! Sometimes, I like to stir a
couple of tablespoons of crème fraîche into the gravy before
serving.

2 tbsp oil
1kg/2¼ lb rolled lean beef, such as brisket
1 onion, sliced
3 celery stalks, sliced
450g/1 lb potatoes, cut into large cubes
8 small carrots
4 small parsnips
600ml/1 pt stock
Salt and freshly ground black pepper
1 tbsp Worcestershire sauce
2 tbsp tomato purée

1. Heat the oil in the open pressure cooker, add the beef
   and cook over high heat, turning frequently, until
   browned all over. Lift out.

2. Add the onion and celery to the pan and cook, stirring
   occasionally, until softened but not browned.

3. Stir in the remaining ingredients and stand the beef on
   top.

4. Fit the lid, bring to High pressure and cook for 30
   minutes.

5. Reduce the pressure quickly in cold water.

6. Lift out the beef and place on a large warmed serving
   dish. Arrange the vegetables around the beef and serve
   the gravy separately.

BARBECUE-STYLE SPARE RIBS

Serves 4   *15 minutes at High pressure*

Choose short ribs if you can, or ask your butcher to cut them for you. I like to serve them with freshly cooked rice and a dressed green salad.

Sauce:
1 medium onion, finely chopped
1 green pepper, seeds removed and finely chopped
400g can chopped tomatoes
2 tbsp wine vinegar
1 tbsp Worcestershire sauce
1 tsp dry mustard powder
½ tsp salt
Few drops of hot chilli sauce

1 tbsp oil
1-1.5kg/2¼-3¼ lb pork spare ribs

1. Put the sauce ingredients into a processor or blender and purée until smooth.

2. Heat the oil in the open pressure cooker, add the ribs and cook, turning occasionally, until well browned. Lift out and drain off any fat.

3. Return the spare ribs to the pan and pour the sauce over.

4. Fit the lid, bring to High pressure and cook for 15 minutes.

5. Reduce the pressure quickly in cold water.

SWEET AND SOUR PORK

Serves 4   *15 minutes at High pressure*

A favourite with children and adults alike, Sweet and Sour Pork is lovely served on a bed of freshly cooked rice.

2 tbsp oil
675g/1½ lb lean pork, cut into cubes
340g can pineapple chunks in syrup
4 tbsp wine vinegar
85g/3 oz brown sugar
1 tbsp soy sauce
½ tsp salt
1 medium onion, finely sliced
1 green pepper, seeds removed and finely sliced
2 tbsp cornflour

1. Heat the oil in the open pressure cooker, add the pork and cook, stirring occasionally until browned.

2. Drain the pineapple, reserving the syrup. Add sufficient water to the syrup to make 300ml/½ pt and pour over the pork. Add the vinegar, sugar, soy sauce, salt, onion and pepper. Bring to the boil, stirring to dissolve the sugar.

3. Fit the lid, bring to High pressure and cook for 15 minutes.

4. Reduce the pressure quickly in cold water.

5. Mix the cornflour with 3 tbsp cold water to make a smooth paste. Stir into the pork with the pineapple chunks. Bring to the boil, stirring, until thickened.

PORK WITH LEMON AND OLIVES

Serves 4   *15 minutes at High pressure*

Accompany this dish with some wide ribbon pasta. A salad of sliced tomatoes and red onion would be good too.

2 tbsp oil
1 medium onion, finely chopped
675g/1½ lb lean pork, cut into cubes
300ml/½ pt dry white wine
Finely grated rind of 1 lemon
Juice of ½ lemon
¼ tsp dried tarragon
Salt and freshly ground black pepper
About 12 pitted black olives

1.   Heat the oil in the open pressure cooker, add the onion and cook, stirring occasionally until softened but not browned

2.   Add the pork and cook, stirring occasionally, until browned.

3.   Stir in the remaining ingredients except the olives.

4.   Fit the lid, bring to High pressure and cook for 15 minutes.

5.   Reduce the pressure quickly in cold water.

6.   Add the olives and adjust the seasoning to taste before serving.

BACON AND BEANS

Serves 4   *25 minutes at High pressure*

Try serving this with hot garlic bread.

225g/8 oz dried haricot beans
25g/1 oz butter
1 medium onion, chopped
1 garlic clove, crushed
1 red pepper, seeds removed and chopped
675g/1½ lb lean bacon joint, cut into cubes
400g can tomatoes
150ml/¼ pt bacon or chicken stock
1 tsp brown sugar
1 tbsp Worcestershire sauce
1 tsp dry mustard powder
1 bay leaf
Salt and freshly ground black pepper

1. Put the beans in a deep bowl and cover with 600ml/1 pt boiling water. Leave to soak for 1 hour.

2. Melt the butter in the open pressure cooker, add the onion and cook, stirring occasionally, until softened but not browned.

3. Add the remaining ingredients, seasoning only lightly with salt. Drain the beans and stir in.

4. Fit the lid, slowly bring to High pressure and cook for 25 minutes.

5. Reduce pressure quickly in cold water. Adjust the seasoning to taste before serving.

BOILED BACON

12 minutes per 450g/1 lb
at High pressure

Pressure cooking is ideal for joints of bacon. The vegetables, herbs and spices add extra flavour.

1 bacon joint
2 carrots, cut into chunks
2 celery sticks, broken in half
1 bay leaf
Sprig of fresh herb, such as thyme, rosemary or sage
6 black peppercorns
3 whole cloves
55g/2 oz toasted breadcrumbs (optional)

1. Weigh the meat and calculate the cooking time (see table on page 44). Put in the open pressure cooker, without the trivet. Cover with cold water and bring to the boil. Remove the bacon, discard the water and rinse the pan.

2. Return the meat to the pan and add the cooking water (see table, page 44), vegetables, herbs and spices.

3. Fit the lid, bring to High pressure and cook for 12 minutes per 450g/1 lb.

4. Reduce the pressure slowly at room temperature.

5. Lift the meat on to a warmed serving dish (strain the cooking liquid and reserve for use as stock).

6. Either serve hot or leave to cool, remove the skin and coat with the toasted breadcrumbs, if using.

BACON IN CIDER

Serves 4–6   *30 minutes at High pressure*

A potato or root vegetable mash goes well with this to soak up the delicious sauce. I like to serve a green vegetable too.

1kg/2¼ lb lean bacon joint
425ml/¾ pt cider
1 medium onion, sliced
2 celery sticks, sliced
6 black peppercorns
A few fresh sage leaves or a pinch of dried sage
2 tbsp cornflour

1. Put the meat in the open pressure cooker, without the trivet. Cover with cold water and bring to the boil. Remove the bacon, discard the water and rinse the pan.

2. Return the bacon to the pan and add the cider, onion, celery, peppercorns and sage.

3. Fit the lid, bring to High pressure and cook for 30 minutes.

4. Reduce the pressure quickly in cold water.

5. Lift the bacon on to a warmed serving dish. Remove the peppercorns. Mix the cornflour with 3 tbsp cold water to make a smooth paste and stir into the sauce. Bring to the boil, stirring continuously, until thickened.

6. Spoon some of the sauce over the bacon and serve the remainder separately.

DEVON LAMB AND POTATO PIE

Serves 4   *13 minutes at High pressure*

This is comfort food that is meant for serving straight from
the pressure cooker on to ready-waiting plates.

25g/1 oz butter
4 large, lean lamb chops
1 large onion, finely chopped
1kg/2¼ lb potatoes, sliced
Salt and freshly ground black pepper
2 cooking apples, peeled and sliced
2 tsp brown sugar
300ml/½ pt dry cider or apple juice
Finely chopped fresh parsley, to serve

1.   Melt the butter in the open pressure cooker, add the
      chops and quickly brown on both sides. Lift out.

2.   Arrange the onion in a layer in the base of the pan. Cover
      with half the potatoes and season. Cover with the apple,
      sprinkle with the sugar and top with the remaining
      potatoes. Lay the chops on top, season and pour the cider
      over.

3.   Fit the lid, bring to High pressure and cook for 13
      minutes.

4.   Reduce the pressure quickly in cold water.

5.   Serve sprinkled with parsley.

LANCASHIRE HOTPOT

Serves 4   *15 minutes at High pressure*

Another warming dish that's absolutely full of flavour. Serve
it in shallow bowls with crusty bread and a green salad.

1kg/2¼ lb potatoes, sliced
Salt and freshly ground black pepper
1 large onion, sliced
225g/8 oz carrots, sliced
2 celery sticks, sliced
675g/1½ lb lean stewing lamb, such as neck, cut into
  cubes
300ml/½ pt lamb or vegetable stock
Chopped fresh herbs, such as parsley, to serve

1. Arrange half the potatoes in the base of the pressure
    cooker, without the trivet. Season and cover with the
    onion, carrots and celery. Arrange the lamb on top.
    Cover with the remaining potatoes. Season and pour
    over the stock.

2. Fit the lid, bring to High pressure and cook for 15
    minutes.

3. Reduce the pressure quickly in cold water.

4. Serve sprinkled with fresh herbs.

LAMB WITH CINNAMON AND APRICOTS

Serves 4   *15 minutes at High pressure*

Couscous makes the ideal accompaniment for this dish – and it's quick to prepare too.

675g/1½ lb lean boned leg of lamb, cut into cubes
1 tbsp flour
2 tbsp olive oil
1 medium onion, chopped
300ml/½ pt lamb or vegetable stock
2 tbsp tomato purée
2 tsp ground cinnamon
115g/4 oz dried apricots
1 tsp sugar
Salt and freshly ground black pepper
2 tbsp toasted pine nuts

1. Toss the lamb in the flour (this is easy to do in a freezer bag).

2. Heat the oil in the open pressure cooker, add the onion and cook, stirring occasionally, until softened but not browned.

3. Add the lamb and cook, stirring occasionally, until browned.

4. Stir in the stock, tomato purée, cinnamon, apricots, sugar and seasoning.

5. Fit the lid, bring to High pressure and cook for 15 minutes.

6. Reduce the pressure quickly in cold water.

7. Serve with the toasted pine nuts sprinkled over.

LIVER AND ONIONS

Serves 4   *5 minutes at High pressure*

The quickest dish of melt-in-the mouth liver and onions you'll ever make!

675g/1½ lb lamb's liver, sliced
25g/1 oz flour
2 tbsp oil
4 streaky bacon rashers, halved crossways
3 medium onions, sliced
300ml/½ pt chicken or vegetable stock
Salt and freshly ground black pepper

1.   Toss the liver in the flour (this is easy to do in a freezer bag).

2.   Heat the oil in the open pressure cooker, add the bacon and fry until crisp. Lift out and keep warm.

3.   Add the onions to the pan and cook, stirring occasionally, until golden brown.

4.   Add the liver and cook, stirring occasionally, until browned.

5.   Stir in the stock and seasoning.

6.   Fit the lid, bring to High pressure and cook for 5 minutes.

7.   Reduce the pressure quickly in cold water.

8.   Serve topped with the crisp bacon.

COUNTRY LIVER PÂTÉ

Serves 4–6   *30 minutes at High pressure*

Serve as a starter or snack, with crusty bread and salad.

6 lean streaky bacon rashers, rinds removed
225g/8 oz pig's liver, sliced
115g/4 oz pork sausage meat
1 medium onion, finely chopped
1 garlic clove, finely chopped
85g/3 oz fresh breadcrumbs
½ tsp salt
Freshly ground black pepper
½ tsp dried sage
1 medium egg, beaten
1 tbsp sherry or brandy

1. Using the back of a knife, stretch the bacon and use it to line a small loaf tin, allowing it to fall loosely over the sides.

2. In a processor or blender, whizz all the remaining ingredients together. (Alternatively, mince the liver finely and mix thoroughly with the remaining ingredients.)

3. Spoon the mixture into the lined tin and fold the ends of the bacon over the pâté. Cover securely with greased foil.

4. Put 600ml/1 pt water into the pressure cooker and add the trivet. Stand the loaf tin on the trivet. Fit the lid, bring to High pressure and cook for 30 minutes.

5. Reduce the pressure slowly at room temperature.

6. Remove the tin from the pressure cooker, loosen the foil slightly, top with a heavy weight and leave until cold. Turn out and serve.

3

POULTRY AND GAME

Chicken is reasonably priced and extremely versatile. It can be pressure cooked whole or in joints, in a variety of sauces, in a remarkably short time.

The tenderising effect of pressure cooking is invaluable when cooking poultry and game. A rabbit or pheasant of dubious age, 'bagged' during a day's shooting, can be a mixed blessing if it turns out to be as tough as old boots! This chapter includes a variety of recipes for the more common types of poultry and game, and a table giving typical cooking times to help you adapt your own favourites.

Adapting recipes

The trivet: This is not used when cooking casseroles, but may be used when pot roasting.

Pressure: Use High pressure and, in general, reduce the pressure quickly after cooking (unless the recipe includes a large quantity of liquid or states otherwise).

Quantity, Thickening and Liquid: See the tips on page 44 in Chapter 2.

Time: Follow the times given in the table. Chicken portions vary in size, therefore I recommend a cooking time of 7–10 minutes, depending on the thickness of the joints. Poultry and game may be stuffed, but remember to weigh the bird after stuffing when calculating the cooking time.

Pot roasting: Follow the general method for Chicken Pot Roast on page 70, varying the time according to the table below.

Freezing: All frozen poultry and game must be completely thawed before pressure cooking. When reheating cooked recipes from frozen, make sure that the food is piping hot before serving. Follow the same advice and method for reheating as given in Chapter 2, page 45.

Cooking times at High pressure	
CHICKEN, poussin	4–7 minutes
roasting, whole	7 minutes per 450g/1 lb
roasting, joints	7–10 minutes
boiling, whole	10 minutes per 450g/1 lb
boiling, joints	15–20 minutes
DUCKLING, whole	12–15 minutes per 450g/1 lb
joints	10–12 minutes
GROUSE, young	10 minutes
old	15 minutes

Cooking times at High pressure	
HARE, joints *Minimum 600ml/1 pt liquid required*	35–40 minutes
RABBIT, joints	20–25 minutes
PARTRIDGE	7–10 minutes
PHEASANT, whole, joints	7–10 minutes
PIGEONS, halved	20–25 minutes
VENISON	20–25 minutes per 450g/1 lb

CHICKEN LIVER PÂTÉ

Serves 6–8   *30 minutes at High pressure*

This is suitable for serving simply with chunks of crusty bread or with melba toast as a starter to a special dinner. It can be made in advance and frozen for up to four weeks.

350g/12 oz chicken livers
1 garlic clove, crushed
1 medium egg, beaten
2 tbsp single cream
1 tbsp chopped fresh mixed herbs or ½ tsp dried mixed
  herbs
1 tsp salt
Freshly ground black pepper
1 tbsp sherry
2 bay leaves
55g/2 oz butter, melted

1. In a processor or blender, whizz together all the ingredients, except the bay leaves and butter.

2. Spoon the mixture into an ovenproof soufflé dish and cover securely with greased foil.

3. Put 600ml/1 pt water into the pressure cooker and add the trivet. Stand the dish on the trivet. Fit the lid, bring to High pressure and cook for 30 minutes.

4. Reduce the pressure slowly at room temperature.

5. Leave to cool, then top with the bay leaves and pour over the melted butter to cover the surface completely. Serve chilled.

CHICKEN AND PINEAPPLE CURRY

Follow the recipe for Curried Beef (page 48) replacing the beef with chicken. Add a small can of pineapple chunks, using the juice as part of the liquid in the recipe and stirring in the pineapple just before serving.

CHICKEN WITH TARRAGON AND LEMON

Follow the recipe for Chicken Pot Roast (page 70). Sprinkle 1 tsp dried tarragon over the chicken in step 2, together with the grated rind of 1 lemon. Add the juice of half the lemon to the stock in step 6.

CHICKEN POT ROAST

Serves 4–6   *7 minutes per 450g/1 lb at High pressure*

You could add small whole potatoes and carrots to this dish. Simply reduce the pressure 7 minutes before the end of the cooking time, add the vegetables, bringing back to High pressure and cook for a further 7 minutes.

**15g/½ oz butter
1 tbsp oil
1.5kg/3 lb 5 oz chicken
300ml/½ pt chicken stock
1 small onion, chopped
1 medium carrot, chopped
1 bay leaf
Salt and freshly ground black pepper
1 tbsp cornflour**

1. Heat the butter and oil in the open pressure cooker, add the chicken and brown quickly on all sides, turning it occasionally. Lift out and drain off any excess fat.

2. Pour the stock into the pan and add the trivet. Stand the chicken on the trivet and add the remaining ingredients except the cornflour.

3. Fit the lid, bring to High pressure and cook for 7 minutes per 450g/1 lb.

4. Reduce the pressure quickly in cold water.

5. Lift out the chicken and keep warm.

6. Strain the stock, discarding the flavouring ingredients and return to the pan. Blend the cornflour with 2 tbsp cold water to make a smooth paste. Stir into the stock and bring to the boil, stirring, until thickened. Adjust the seasoning to taste.

7. Serve the sauce with the chicken.

CHICKEN WITH SUMMER VEGETABLES

Serves 4   *7–10 minutes at High pressure*

Accompany this with some bread to mop up the juices.

1 tbsp olive oil
12 whole baby onions or shallots, skinned
8 chicken thighs, or thighs and drumsticks
1 red, yellow or orange pepper, seeds removed and cut into strips
550g/1¼ lb mixed fresh vegetables, such as baby salad potatoes, carrots, sweetcorn, courgettes, green beans and sugar snap peas
150ml/¼ pt chicken stock
1 tbsp tomato purée
Finely grated rind and juice of ½ lemon (use the remaining half as a garnish if wished)
2 tbsp chopped fresh herbs such as thyme, parsley or chives
Salt and freshly ground black pepper
115g/4 oz baby tomatoes, halved

1. Heat the oil in the open pressure cooker, add the onions and cook, stirring occasionally, until slightly softened but not browned.

2. Add the chicken and brown quickly on all sides.

3. Stir in the remaining ingredients, except the tomatoes.

4. Fit the lid, bring to High pressure and cook for 7–10 minutes.

5. Reduce the pressure quickly in cold water.

6. Adjust the seasoning to taste and stir in the tomatoes. Bubble gently in the open pan for 1–2 minutes until the tomatoes are slightly softened and serve garnished with lemon, if using.

COQ AU VIN

Serves 4   *7–10 minutes at High pressure*

This tasty and sophisticated meal is perfect for quick week-day meals, or equally for formal dining. Serve this classic French dish with buttered tagliatelli and a fresh and crispy green salad. For the full, authentic French effect, don't forget to serve a glass (or two) of red wine!

25g/1 oz butter
4 streaky bacon rashers, cut into strips
8 boned chicken thighs
16 baby onions
115g/4 oz button mushrooms
2 garlic cloves, crushed
150ml/¼ pt chicken stock
150ml/¼ pt dry red wine
Salt and freshly ground black pepper
1 bay leaf
1 tbsp cornflour
2 tbsp brandy
Chopped fresh parsley

1. Melt the butter in the open pressure cooker.

2. Add the bacon and cook, stirring occasionally, until just starting to brown.

3. Add the chicken and cook quickly, stirring occasionally, until evenly browned all over.

4. Stir in the onions, mushrooms, garlic, stock, wine, seasoning and bay leaf.

5. Fit the lid, bring to High pressure and cook for 7–10 minutes.

6. Reduce the pressure quickly in cold water.

7. Remove the bay leaf.

8.   Using a slotted spoon, lift out the chicken and keep warm.

9.   Blend the cornflour with the brandy to make a smooth paste and stir into the sauce in the pan. Bring to the boil, stirring continuously, until thickened.

10.   Adjust the seasoning to taste and pour over the chicken.

11.   Sprinkle with parsley to serve.

RICE WITH CHICKEN AND HERBS

Serves 4   *8 minutes at High pressure*

You could use Italian risotto rice, such as Arborio, in place of ordinary long grain rice to give a creamy consistency.

25g/1 oz butter
1 tbsp olive oil
1 medium onion, chopped
1 celery stalk, thinly sliced
175g/6 oz long grain rice
600ml/1 pt chicken stock
3 tbsp chopped mixed fresh herbs or 1 tbsp dried
350g/12 oz chicken, cut into small slices
Salt and freshly ground black pepper
115g/4 oz frozen peas

1. Heat the butter and oil in the open pressure cooker, add the onion and celery and cook, stirring occasionally, until softened but not browned.

2. Add the rice and cook, stirring, for 2–3 minutes.

3. Stir in the remaining ingredients, except the peas, and bring to the boil, stirring continuously.

4. Fit the lid, bring to High pressure over medium heat and cook for 8 minutes.

5. Reduce the pressure slowly at room temperature.

6. Remove the lid, stir in the frozen peas and cook gently for about 3–5 minutes, stirring gently and fluffing up the rice.

7. Serve immediately.

CHICKEN MARENGO

Serves 4   *7–10 minutes at High pressure*

This is good served with freshly cooked rice.

1 tbsp olive oil
1 medium onion, thinly sliced
4 chicken quarters
4 tomatoes, skinned and quartered
115g/4 oz button mushrooms
300ml/½ pt dry white wine or vermouth
1 garlic clove, crushed
Bouquet garni
Salt and freshly ground black pepper
1 tbsp cornflour
2 tbsp brandy

1. Heat the oil in the open pressure cooker, add the onion and cook, stirring occasionally, until softened but not browned.

2. Add the chicken and brown quickly on all sides.

3. Stir in the tomatoes, mushrooms, wine, garlic, bouquet garni and seasoning.

4. Fit the lid, bring to High pressure and cook for 7–10 minutes.

5. Reduce the pressure quickly in cold water.

6. Using a slotted spoon, lift the chicken on to a hot serving dish and keep warm. Remove the bouquet garni.

7. Blend the cornflour with the brandy to make a smooth paste and stir into the sauce in the pan. Bring to the boil, stirring continuously, until thickened. Adjust the seasoning to taste.

8. Pour the sauce over the chicken to serve.

SPICED CHICKEN WITH CASHEW NUTS

Serves 4   *7–10 minutes at High pressure*

2 tbsp oil
1 medium onion, sliced
1 garlic clove, crushed
1 tsp chilli powder
1 tsp ground ginger
1 tbsp curry powder
300ml/½ pt chicken stock
8 chicken thighs, skinned
3 tbsp natural yogurt
115g/4 oz cashew nuts, toasted

1. Heat the oil in the open pressure cooker, add the onion and garlic and cook, stirring occasionally, until softened but not browned.

2. Add the chilli powder, ginger and curry powder, and cook over a low heat for 2 minutes, stirring.

3. Stir in the chicken stock and add the chicken.

4. Fit the lid, bring to High pressure and cook for 7–10 minutes.

5. Reduce pressure quickly in cold water.

6. Just before serving swirl in the yogurt and scatter the cashew nuts over the top (don't be tempted to reheat it or the yogurt will separate).

CHICKEN IN A CREAM SAUCE

Serves 4   *20 minutes total at High pressure*

This recipe is ideal for thick turkey pieces too. I like to serve
it with rice or tagliatelle.

1 tbsp oil
4 chicken portions
300ml/½ pt chicken stock
1 tbsp chopped fresh herbs, such as parsley, thyme or
   tarragon
Salt and freshly ground black pepper
16 baby onions, peeled
115g/4 oz button mushrooms
Finely grated rind and juice of ½ lemon
2 tsp cornflour
150ml/¼ pt double cream

1.   Heat the oil in the open pressure cooker, add the chicken
     and cook, turning occasionally, until browned.

2.   Add the stock, herbs and seasoning.

3.   Fit the lid, bring to High pressure and cook for 15
     minutes.

4.   Reduce the pressure quickly in cold water.

5.   Add the onions, mushrooms, lemon rind and juice.

6.   Fit the lid, bring to pressure and cook for a further 5
     minutes.

7.   Reduce the pressure quickly in cold water.

8.   Stir the cornflour into the cream and add to the pressure
     cooker. Heat gently, stirring, until the sauce comes to the
     boil and has thickened slightly.

RAGOÛT OF VENISON

Serves 4–6   *30 minutes at High pressure*

Today there are plenty of venison farms to supply us with this
very lean and delicious meat. Because it has so little fat it can
be dry, so I like to marinate it.

1 medium onion, finely chopped
1 tsp salt
6 black peppercorns, crushed
1 bay leaf
6 tbsp olive oil
3 tbsp dry red wine
1kg/2¼ lb casserole venison, cut into bite-size pieces
85g/3 oz pancetta cubes or chopped streaky bacon
2 medium onions, chopped
2 medium carrots, chopped
300ml/½ pt dry red wine
1 tbsp fresh thyme leaves or 1 tsp dried
Salt and freshly ground black pepper
2 tbsp cornflour

1.   Put the first six ingredients into a shallow non-metal
     container, add the venison and toss until well coated.
     Cover and leave to marinate for about 2 hours, turning
     the venison occasionally.

2.   Heat the open pressure cooker, add the pancetta and
     cook, stirring occasionally, until the fat begins to run
     and it starts to brown.

3.   With a slotted spoon, lift the venison from the mari-
     nade and pat dry with kitchen paper. Add it to the
     pressure cooker and cook over high heat, stirring until
     browned.

4. Stir in the onions, carrots, wine, thyme, salt and pepper.

5. Fit the lid, bring to High pressure and cook for 30 minutes.

6. Reduce the pressure quickly in cold water.

7. Strain the marinade, discarding the solids, and blend in the cornflour to make a smooth paste. Stir into the venison and heat, stirring, until the mixture comes to the boil and has thickened.

PHEASANT WITH GRAPES IN WINE AND CREAM SAUCE

Serves 4   *7–10 minutes at High pressure*

Good served with pan-fried potatoes and a green vegetable such as broccoli.

25g/1 oz butter
1 large or 2 small pheasants
1 medium onion, finely chopped
2 celery stalks, sliced
150ml/¼ pt chicken stock
150ml/¼ pt dry white wine
Bouquet garni
Salt and black pepper
225g/8 oz seedless green grapes, halved
4 tbsp double cream or crème fraîche

1. Melt the butter in the open pressure cooker, add the pheasant(s) and brown quickly on all sides. Lift out of the pressure cooker and drain off excess fat.

2. Add the onion and celery to the pressure cooker and cook, stirring occasionally, until softened but not browned.

3. Add the pheasant(s), stock, wine, bouquet garni, salt and pepper.

4. Fit the lid, bring to High pressure and cook for 7 minutes (small pheasants) or 10 minutes (large pheasant).

5. Reduce the pressure quickly in cold water.

6. Remove the bouquet garni. Add the grapes and cream and heat through until bubbling. Adjust the seasoning to taste and serve.

4

FISH

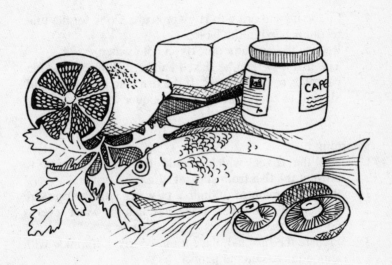

Time saving is not the big advantage when pressure cooking fish; indeed, conventional methods don't take much longer. The main advantage is that only the minimum liquid is usually required and this helps reduce loss of flavour. Furthermore, the smell of fish is trapped inside the pressure cooker until the end of cooking.

Most fish recipes are improved with the addition of a good home-made fish stock – see page 35.

The following cooking methods can be adapted to pressure cooking.

Poaching
1. The trivet is not used.
2. Prepare the fish and place it in the pressure cooker.
3. Add a minimum of 300ml/½ pt liquid. This may be lightly salted water with a teaspoon of lemon juice, or wine or cider. If the poaching liquid is to be used as the basis of a sauce, sliced vegetables and herbs can be included to give extra flavour. A mixture of half milk to water is good for smoked fish with no salt added.
4. Fit the lid and bring to High pressure. Cook for the time recommended in the table.
5. Reduce the pressure quickly in cold water.
6. The fish may then be flaked and served in a sauce, pie, pancakes or pastry cases. If the fish is to be served cold, allow it to cool in the poaching liquor.

Steaming
1. Use the trivet, which should be lightly greased to prevent the fish from sticking.
2. Put a minimum of 300ml/½ pt water into the pressure cooker with the trivet. Make sure that the water level is no higher than the trivet.
3. Prepare the fish and place it on the trivet. Sprinkle with lemon juice, salt and pepper.
4. Fit the lid and bring to High pressure. Cook for the time recommended in the table.
5. Reduce the pressure quickly in cold water.

En papillote (in a packet)
1. Use the trivet.
2. Prepare the fish and place it on a greased square of foil. It can be seasoned and dotted with butter, stuffed or sprinkled with finely sliced vegetables, such as onion, mushrooms or celery. The foil should then be folded over the fish and sealed to form a secure parcel.

3. Put 300ml/½ pt water into the pressure cooker with the trivet.
4. Place the parcel on the trivet, fit the lid and bring to High pressure. Cook for the time recommended in the table.
5. Reduce the pressure quickly in cold water.

Stewing/Casseroling

1. The trivet is not used.
2. Prepare the fish and cut it into chunks.
3. An onion and other vegetables may be sautéed in butter or margarine in the open pressure cooker. As fish takes such a short time to pressure cook, ensure that root vegetables, such as potatoes and carrots, are thinly sliced to cook within the allotted time.
4. Add the fish, some lemon juice and at least 300ml/½ pt stock, wine or cider. Add herbs and seasoning.
5. Fit the lid and bring to High pressure. Cook for the time recommended in the table.
6. Reduce the pressure quickly in cold water.

Braising

Follow the general method for stewing, except that the fish is cooked whole on the greased trivet, which is placed on top of the vegetables and raised above the liquid. The vegetables can be puréed afterwards to make a sauce.

Cooking times at High pressure Times will vary depending on the thickness of the fish.		
	Steaks or fillets	*Whole*
Bass, bream, brill, cod, coley, haddock, hake, halibut, ling, monkfish, plaice, skate, sole, turbot, whiting	3–6 minutes	5–6 minutes per 450g/1 lb
Herrings, mackerel, mullet, trout	3–6 minutes	5–8 minutes
Salmon	3–6 minutes	8–12 minutes per 450g/1 lb
Lobster		10 minutes
Crab		7–10 minutes
Prawns, shrimps		2–3 minutes

Frozen fish
There is no need to thaw frozen fish before cooking, unless it is to be stuffed. Cooking times are the same as for fresh fish.

SMOKED MACKEREL KEDGEREE

Serves 4   *8 minutes at High pressure*

This tasty variation of the traditional recipe uses smoked mackerel which doesn't need cooking in advance.

25g/1 oz butter
1 small onion, finely chopped
175g/6 oz long grain rice
600ml/1 pt vegetable stock
450g/1 lb smoked mackerel fillets, skin removed and
  flaked
2 tbsp cream
4 hard-boiled eggs, shells removed and sliced
Chopped fresh parsley

1. Melt the butter in the open pressure cooker, add the onion and cook, stirring occasionally, until softened but not browned.

2. Add the rice and stir over a low heat for a couple of minutes.

3. Add the stock and bring to the boil, stirring continuously.

4. Reduce the heat to a medium setting, fit the lid, bring to High pressure and cook for 8 minutes.

5. Reduce the pressure slowly at room temperature.

6. Gently fold in the mackerel and egg. Add the cream and stir gently over a low heat until piping hot. Serve immediately.

COD PROVENÇALE

Serves 4   *4 minutes at High pressure*

This is good served with thick slices of toasted French bread.

1 tbsp olive oil
1 medium onion, finely chopped
1 garlic clove, crushed
675g/1½ lb thick cod fillet, cut into 4 portions
400g can chopped tomatoes
1 green pepper, seeds removed and chopped
1 tbsp tomato purée
½ tsp brown sugar
1 bay leaf
Salt and freshly ground black pepper
1 tablespoon chopped fresh parsley

1. Heat the oil in the open pressure cooker, add the onion and cook, stirring occasionally, until softened but not browned.

2. Add the remaining ingredients, except the parsley.

3. Fit the lid, bring to High pressure and cook for 4 minutes.

4. Reduce the pressure quickly with cold water.

5. Remove the bay leaf before serving and sprinkle with parsley.

DEVON FISH CASSEROLE

Serves 4   *4 minutes at High pressure*

I like to serve this in bowls accompanied by hunks of crusty bread.

25g/1 oz butter
1 medium onion, finely chopped
450g/1 lb skinless white fish, such as whiting or haddock, cut into chunks
225g/8 oz peeled prawns, thawed if frozen
225g/8 oz button mushrooms, sliced
Juice of ½ lemon
300ml/½ pt dry cider
Salt and freshly ground black pepper
½ tsp fresh thyme leaves or a pinch of dried
150ml/¼ pt double cream or crème fraîche

1. Melt the butter in the open pressure cooker, add the onion and cook, stirring occasionally, until softened but not browned.

2. Add the fish, prawns, mushrooms, lemon juice, cider, seasoning and thyme.

3. Fit the lid, bring to High pressure and cook for 4 minutes.

4. Reduce the pressure quickly in cold water.

5. Add the cream and heat gently until the sauce bubbles and thickens slightly.

SALMON PUDDING

Serves 4   *15 minutes steaming*
                                        25 minutes at Low pressure

This recipe is great for using left-over mashed potato and ingredients from the store cupboard. Serve the pudding straight from the basin and accompany it with a crunchy salad.

220g can salmon, drained, thick bones removed and
   flaked
1 small onion, finely chopped
225g/8 oz mashed potato
55g/2 oz fresh breadcrumbs
1 tbsp chopped fresh chives
1 medium egg, beaten
2 tbsp milk
55g/2 oz butter, melted
1 tsp Worcestershire sauce
Salt and freshly ground black pepper

1.   Butter a 1 litre/1¾ pt pudding basin.

2.   Combine all the ingredients and spoon the mixture into the basin. Cover securely with a double layer of grease-proof paper or aluminium foil.

3.   Put 850ml/1½ pt water into the pressure cooker with the trivet. Stand the basin on the trivet.

4.   Fit the lid and, without adding the weight, and without bringing to High pressure, steam gently for 15 minutes.

5.   Bring to Low pressure and cook for 25 minutes.

6.   Reduce the pressure slowly at room temperature.

TROUT WITH BUTTERY ALMONDS

Serves 4   *8 minutes at High pressure*

Serve each person with a foil parcel so he or she can tear it open and appreciate the wonderful aroma that wafts out.

**4 whole trout, each weighing about 225g/8 oz, cleaned
    and heads removed
1 tbsp lemon juice
Salt and freshly ground pepper
115g/4 oz butter
55g/2 oz flaked almonds**

1. Place each trout on a buttered square of foil, large enough to enclose it completely. Sprinkle each trout with lemon juice and seasoning.

2. Melt the butter in a small pan, add the almonds and cook, stirring occasionally, until slightly browned. Spoon the almonds and butter over the trout. Fold the foil over the trout and seal each parcel securely.

3. Put 300ml/½ pt water into the pressure cooker with the trivet. Lay the parcels on the trivet.

4. Fit the lid, bring to High pressure and cook for 8 minutes.

5. Reduce the pressure quickly in cold water.

SOUSED HERRINGS

Serves 4   *6 minutes at High pressure*

If you are lucky enough to be able to buy your herrings from a fishmonger, ask him (or her) to prepare and bone them for you. Otherwise, look for boneless fillets.

16 herring fillets, bones removed
Salt and freshly ground black pepper
1 blade of mace
8 black peppercorns
2 small onions, thinly sliced
1 bay leaf
150ml/¼ pt malt vinegar

1. Sprinkle the cut side of each herring fillet with salt and pepper. Roll up from the tail end with the skin side outwards. Secure with cocktail sticks.

2. Put into the pressure cooker without the trivet. Add the remaining ingredients plus 150ml/¼ pt water.

3. Fit the lid, bring to High pressure and cook for 6 minutes.

4. Reduce the pressure quickly in cold water.

5. Lift the herrings into a serving dish and remove the cocktail sticks. Spoon the remaining mixture over them and allow to cool before serving.

WHITE FISH IN CAPER SAUCE

Serves 4   *4 minutes at High pressure*

Capers come in salt or in vinegar. Whichever you choose, wash them thoroughly and drain them before use.

1 bunch of spring onions, chopped
675g/1½ lb white fish fillets, such as whiting, cod or
  haddock, skinned
1 tbsp capers
Salt and freshly ground black pepper
150ml/¼ pt fish or vegetable stock
150ml/¼ pt milk, plus 1 tbsp extra
1 tbsp cornflour

1. Sprinkle the onions over the base of the pressure cooker, without the trivet. Add the fish and sprinkle with capers and seasoning. Pour the stock and milk over.

2. Fit the lid, bring to High pressure and cook for 4 minutes.

3. Reduce the pressure quickly in cold water.

4. Blend the cornflour with the extra 1 tbsp milk to make a smooth paste.

5. Using a slotted spoon, lift the fish on to a serving dish and keep warm.

6. Add the cornflour paste to the sauce in the pressure cooker and heat, stirring, until it comes to the boil and thickens. Pour over the fish and serve.

MACKEREL WITH GOOSEBERRY SAUCE

Serves 4   *8 minutes at High pressure*

**4 mackerel, each weighing about 225g/8 oz, cleaned and
  heads removed**
25g/1 oz butter, melted
1 tsp lemon juice
Salt and freshly ground pepper
225g/8 oz fresh or frozen gooseberries
Pinch of grated nutmeg
4 tbsp water
25g/1 oz caster sugar

1. Butter four squares of foil, each large enough to enclose
    one mackerel. Brush the insides of the fish with the
    melted butter and sprinkle with lemon juice, salt and
    pepper. Wrap each mackerel in the foil and seal
    securely.

2. Put the gooseberries, nutmeg and 4 tbsp water into an
    unperforated separator basket or container. Cover
    securely with foil.

3. Put 300ml/½ pt water into the pressure cooker with the
    trivet. Stand the container on the trivet with the parcels
    alongside.

4. Fit the lid, making sure that the parcels do not block any
    air vent. Bring to High pressure and cook for 8 minutes,
    then reduce pressure quickly in cold water.

5. While the gooseberries are still hot, add the sugar and
    stir until dissolved. Either tip into a food processor or
    blender and purée until smooth, or mash with a fork for
    a coarser sauce.

6. Unwrap the fish and serve with the sauce poured over or
    separately.

5

VEGETABLES AND RICE

Vegetables benefit from pressure cooking not only because it saves time, but also because it can reduce the loss of colour, flavour and vitamins which occurs when cooking in a pan of boiling water. The small amount of cooking water used can be added to flavour soups or gravy.

Rice can be cooked either as a plain accompaniment, to serve with curry or other oriental dishes, or together with vegetables, meat or fish as a complete dish.

To cook Rice
1. Put 175g/6 oz long grain rice into an unperforated basket or container.

2. Add 600ml/1 pt salted water and cover securely with greaseproof paper or foil.
3. Put 300ml/½ pt water into the pressure cooker, with the trivet. Stand the container of rice on the trivet.
4. Fit the lid, bring to High pressure and cook for 5 minutes.
5. Reduce the pressure slowly at room temperature.
6. Fluff the rice with a fork before serving.

All in together

A selection of vegetables can be pressure cooked simultaneously. Ideally they should have similar cooking times, otherwise the more delicate vegetables will overcook. If this is not possible, then cut the larger vegetables into smaller pieces to compensate. Medium-size potatoes will cook in a similar time to whole carrots and parsnips. If you prefer your carrots sliced, then the other vegetables should be cut smaller. Mashed potatoes, carrots and runner beans can be cooked at the same time by finely slicing the potato, thinly slicing the carrots and leaving the beans in fairly large lengths.

Cooking Times

Cooking times will depend on the size and quality of the vegetables. Use the cooking times on page 97 as a guide. Remember, whole carrots take longer to cook than sliced; new potatoes need longer than old ones. Individual taste also varies, so if you prefer your vegetables with a 'bite', reduce the cooking times slightly.

Main Course Vegetables

Some of the following recipes are intended as a main course and some could be either a main course or a side vegetable (shown as serving *4* or *2* to indicate that the quantity is sufficient for four as a side dish or two as a main course).

Fresh Vegetables

1. The trivet is used to keep the vegetables above the water.

Use the minimum amount of liquid required – usually 300ml/½ pt or 150ml/¼ pt.

2. Prepare the vegetables, put them into the perforated baskets and stand them on the trivet. If a large quantity of one vegetable is being cooked, pile it straight on to the trivet, making sure the pressure cooker is no more than two thirds full.
3. Fit the lid and bring to High pressure. Cook for the time recommended in the table.
4. Reduce the pressure quickly in cold water.

Dried Beans and Peas
1. With a pressure cooker, long overnight soaking is unnecessary. Lentils require no soaking at all and other vegetables need only one hour.
2. Wash the dried vegetables, cover with boiling water and leave to soak for an hour. Do not use bicarbonate of soda, as it may stain the pressure cooker.
3. The trivet is not required. Pour into the pressure cooker at least 1.2 litres/2 pt liquid, part of which can be made up from the soaking water. This quantity is sufficient for cooking 450g/1 lb of vegetables and should be increased proportionately if more vegetables are to be cooked.
4. Bring the liquid to the boil and add the drained vegetables. Don't fill the pressure cooker more than half full as the liquid tends to froth up during cooking.
5. Reduce the heat to medium, fit the lid and bring to High pressure on this heat. Cook for the time recommended in the table (page 96).
6. Reduce the pressure slowly at room temperature.

Blanching Vegetables for Freezing
1. Blanching vegetables in a pressure cooker is quick, uses little fuel and reduces the steam in the kitchen. Instead of the large pan of boiling water usually needed, use only the minimum amount of liquid required – usually 300ml/½ pt or 150ml/¼ pt.

2.   Prepare the vegetables for freezing, as you would normally.
3.   Put the water into the pressure cooker, together with the trivet, and bring the water to the boil.
4.   Pile the vegetables loosely into the perforated baskets or in a special blanching basket. Don't fill the pressure cooker more than two-thirds full or pack the vegetables too tightly, as this prevents full circulation of the steam.
5.   Fit the lid and bring to Medium pressure. Cook them for times given in the table (page 98). Do not exceed the recommended times or the vegetables will end up cooked rather than blanched.
6.   Reduce the pressure quickly in cold water. Remove the vegetables and immediately plunge them into plenty of cold water to cool quickly. Drain, dry, pack and freeze as usual.

Frozen Vegetables
When pressure cooking frozen vegetables, there is no need to thaw them first. Cook for the time recommended for fresh vegetables.

Cooking times at High pressure for **dried beans and peas**	
Name of Vegetable	*Minutes*
Butter beans	30
Borlotti and Haricot beans, small	20
Haricot beans, large	30
Red Kidney beans	20
Lentils	7
Peas, whole	20
Peas, split	15

*Cooking times at High pressure for **fresh vegetables***	
Name of Vegetable	*Minutes*
Artichokes, globe	6–10
Artichokes, Jerusalem	4–6
Asparagus	2–4
Beans, broad	3–5
Beans, French or runner	3–5
Beetroot, small	10
Beetroot, medium	15–20
Beetroot, large	20–30
Broccoli	3–4
Brussels sprouts	3–4
Cabbage, shredded	3
Carrots, whole	6–7
Carrots, sliced	3–4
Cauliflower, whole	5–8
Cauliflower, florets	3–4
Celery	3
Chicory, whole	3–6
Courgettes, whole	3–4
Courgettes, sliced	1–2
Leeks, whole	4
Leeks, sliced	2
Marrow, thickly sliced	3–4
Onions, sliced	3
Onions, whole	6–10
Parsnips, quartered	5–7
Parsnips, sliced	4
Peas	3–4

Cooking times at High pressure for *fresh vegetables*	
Name of Vegetable	*Minutes*
Peppers, stuffed	5
Potatoes, new, small, whole	6–7
Potatoes, old, whole	12
Potatoes, old, quartered	7
Potatoes, old, sliced	5
Spinach	1–2
Swede, cubed	4
Sweetcorn, whole	3–5
Turnip, sliced	2–3

Blanching Times at Medium pressure	
Type of vegetable	*Minutes*
Artichokes, Jerusalem, cubed	1
Asparagus	bring to pressure only
Beans, broad	1
Beans, French or runner	bring to pressure only
Beetroot, sliced	7
Broccoli	1
Brussels sprouts	1
Carrots	2
Cauliflower, florets	1
Celery, young hearts	2
Celery stalks	1
Courgettes, sliced	bring to pressure only
Chicory	1
Parsnips, sliced	1
Peas	1
Potatoes, new, small	2

Blanching Times at Medium pressure	
Type of vegetable	Minutes
Spinach	bring to pressure only
Swede, sliced	1
Sweetcorn	2
Turnips, small, whole	2

RATATOUILLE

Serves 4 or 2   *5 minutes at High pressure*

Serve this dish, which originates in Provence, hot as a vegetable or cold as a starter.

2 tbsp olive oil
1 medium onion, chopped
1 garlic clove, crushed
1 red pepper, seeds removed and sliced
1 yellow pepper, seeds removed and sliced
1 medium aubergine, sliced
4 large courgettes, thickly sliced
450g/1 lb tomatoes, skinned and quartered
Salt and freshly ground black pepper

1. Heat the oil in the open pressure cooker, add the onion and garlic and cook, stirring occasionally, until softened but not browned.

2. Add the remaining ingredients plus 150ml/¼ pt water.

3. Fit the lid, bring to High pressure and cook for 5 minutes.

4. Reduce pressure quickly in cold water.

5. Adjust the seasoning to taste before serving.

CABBAGE IN A CREAMY SAUCE

Serves 4   *4 minutes at High pressure*

This is particularly good served with boiled ham or with grilled thick sausages.

25g/1 oz butter
1 medium onion, finely chopped
1 small or ½ a large white cabbage, finely shredded
150ml/¼ pt chicken stock
Salt and freshly ground black pepper
Good pinch of grated nutmeg
1 tbsp cornflour
150ml/¼ pt milk

1. Melt the butter in the open pressure cooker, add the onion and cook gently, stirring occasionally, until softened but not browned.

2. Add the cabbage, stock and seasoning, mixing well.

3. Fit the lid, bring to High pressure and cook for 4 minutes.

4. Reduce the pressure quickly in cold water.

5. Blend the cornflour with the milk to make a smooth cream. Stir into the cabbage and bring to the boil, stirring continuously, until thickened.

AMERICAN-STYLE BUTTER BEANS

Serves 4   *30 minutes at High pressure*

450g/1 lb dried butter beans
1 tbsp oil
15g/½ oz butter
115g/4 oz pancetta cubes or chopped streaky bacon
1 medium onion, chopped
400g can chopped tomatoes
1 chicken stock cube
2 tbsp tomato purée
2 tsp sugar
Salt and freshly ground black pepper
1 bay leaf
1 tbsp lemon juice

1. Wash the beans, cover with 1.2 litre/2 pt boiling water and leave to soak for 1 hour.

2. Heat the oil and butter in the open pressure cooker, add the pancetta and cook, stirring occasionally, until start-ing to brown. Add the onion and cook gently until softened but not browned.

3. Drain the beans (reserving the soaking liquid) and add.

4. Tip the can of tomatoes into a measuring jug and make up to 1 litre/1¾ pt with the soaking liquid from the beans. Add this to the pressure cooker, together with the remaining ingredients.

5. Bring to the boil, then reduce the heat to medium. Fit the lid, bring to High pressure and cook for 30 minutes.

6. Reduce the pressure slowly at room temperature.

7. Remove the bay leaf, adjust the seasoning to taste and serve.

RED CABBAGE WITH APPLE

Serves 4   *4 minutes at High pressure*

Based on a German recipe, this dish freezes well. It's good served with sausages and other grilled meats, or try serving it with the turkey roast on Christmas Day.

25g/1 oz butter
1 medium onion, finely chopped
1 small or ½ a large red cabbage, finely shredded
2 cooking apples, peeled, cored and thickly sliced
25g/1 oz sultanas
150ml/¼ pt dry cider or perry
2 tbsp wine vinegar
1 tbsp brown sugar
Salt and freshly ground black pepper

1. Melt the butter in the open pressure cooker, add the onion and cook, stirring occasionally until softened but not browned.

2. Add the remaining ingredients and mix well together.

3. Fit the lid, bring to High pressure and cook for 4 minutes.

4. Reduce the pressure quickly in cold water.

5. Adjust the seasoning to taste before serving and, if wished, bubble in the open pan to reduce the liquid slightly.

GREEN LENTILS WITH PANCETTA AND MUSTARD

Serves 4 or 2   *7 minutes at High pressure*

This dish goes particularly well with fried or grilled white fish. It's good with roast meat or grilled sausages too.

1 tbsp olive oil
115g/4 oz pancetta cubes or chopped streaky bacon
1 medium onion, chopped
1 garlic clove, crushed
225g/8 oz green lentils, washed and drained
600ml/1 pt vegetable stock
Salt and freshly ground black pepper
Bouquet garni
1 tbsp wholegrain mustard

1. Heat the oil in the open pressure cooker, add the pancetta and cook, stirring occasionally, until golden brown.

2. Add the onion and garlic and cook, stirring occasionally, until softened but not browned.

3. Stir in the lentils, stock, seasoning and bouquet garni.

4. Bring to the boil and reduce the heat to medium. Fit the lid, bring to pressure and cook for 7 minutes.

5. Reduce the pressure slowly at room temperature.

6. Remove the bouquet garni, stir in the mustard and adjust the seasoning to taste. Heat through and serve.

FILLED PEPPERS

Serves 4 *7 minutes at High pressure*

Peppers with flat bottoms will stand up during cooking.

1 tbsp oil
1 medium onion, finely chopped
1 garlic clove, crushed
450g/1 lb lean minced beef
115g/4 oz cooked long grain rice
1 tbsp chopped fresh herbs, such as parsley, thyme,
   rosemary, sage
1 tbsp tomato purée
1 tsp Worcestershire sauce
Salt and freshly ground black pepper
4 medium peppers (any colour, equal size)

1. Heat the oil in a saucepan, add the onion and garlic and cook, stirring occasionally, until softened but not browned.

2. Add the beef to the saucepan and cook quickly, stirring occasionally, until browned. Stir in the rice, herbs, purée, sauce and seasoning, mixing well.

3. Cut a shallow lid from the stalk end of each pepper and carefully scoop out the seeds, taking care not to cut through the outer wall. Spoon in the beef mixture.

4. Pour 300ml/½ pt water into the pressure cooker and add the trivet. Stand the peppers upright on the trivet so that they do not touch the walls of the pressure cooker. (To keep them upright, you may like to stand them in an ovenproof dish.)

5. Fit the lid, bring to High pressure and cook for 7 minutes.

6. Holding the pressure cooker level (so the peppers remain upright), reduce the pressure quickly in cold water.

LEEK AND TOMATO CASSEROLE

Serves 4   *3 minutes at High pressure*

This really quick dish is good served with crisp-cooked bacon rashers or bacon chops.

900g/2 lb leeks, cleaned and cut into 2.5cm/1 in lengths
200g can chopped tomatoes
2 tbsp tomato purée
1 tsp sugar
Salt and freshly ground black pepper
1 tbsp lemon juice
2 tbsp chopped fresh parsley

1. Put all the ingredients, except the parsley, into the pressure cooker, without the trivet.

2. Fit the lid, bring to High pressure and cook for 3 minutes.

3. Reduce the pressure quickly in cold water.

4. Adjust the seasoning to taste and stir in the parsley.

'RISOTTO' WITH COURGETTES

Serves 4   *8 minutes at High pressure*

A true risotto is cooked in an open pan, adding the stock a little at a time and stirring continuously for about 20 minutes. I have adapted this recipe to cook in just under half the time in the pressure cooker.

1 tbsp olive oil
1 medium onion, chopped
1 garlic clove, crushed
175g/6 oz risotto rice
4 courgettes, thinly sliced
1 red or yellow pepper, seeds removed and chopped
600ml/1 pt chicken or vegetable stock
1 tbsp tomato purée
Salt and freshly ground black pepper
1 tbsp chopped fresh herbs, such as parsley, oregano or
  thyme
25g/1 oz butter
Freshly grated or shaved Parmesan cheese, to serve

1. Heat the oil in the open pressure cooker, add the onion and garlic and cook, stirring occasionally, until softened but not browned.

2. Add the rice and cook, stirring, for 2–3 minutes. Add the courgettes, pepper, stock, tomato purée and seasoning. Heat, stirring continuously, until the mixture comes to the boil.

3. Reduce the heat to a medium setting, fit the lid, bring to High pressure and cook for 8 minutes.

4. Reduce the pressure slowly at room temperature.

5. Remove the lid and continue to cook over a low heat, stirring and adjusting the seasoning to taste.

6. Stir in the herbs and butter and serve topped with Parmesan cheese.

COURGETTES, PROVENÇAL STYLE

Serves 4   *4 minutes at High pressure*

This tastes good hot or at room temperature. Make it into a main dish for two persons by spooning the cooked mixture into shallow flameproof dishes, topping with grated cheese and grilling until melted and bubbling. Serve with a good crusty loaf of bread.

1 tbsp olive oil
1 medium onion, sliced
1 garlic clove, crushed
900g/2 lb courgettes, cut into 1cm/½ in slices
200g can tomatoes, including juice
Salt and freshly ground black pepper
1 tbsp chopped fresh herbs, such as parsley, thyme or
** oregano**

1.   Heat the oil in the open pressure cooker, add the onion and garlic and cook, stirring occasionally, until softened but not browned.

2.   Stir in the remaining ingredients.

3.   Fit the lid, bring to High pressure and cook for 4 minutes.

4.   Reduce pressure quickly in cold water.

5.   Adjust the seasoning to taste before serving.

6

PUDDINGS

Although a pressure cooker is excellent for steaming traditional sponge and suet puddings, it's also good at cooking more delicate desserts, such as Crème Caramel (page 116) and Filled Peaches with Almonds (page 121).

This chapter includes a variety of steamed puddings, custards and fruit dishes, but if you wish to convert a favourite recipe to pressure cooking, follow these guidelines.

Fresh Fruit

Ripeness and size
When selecting fruit for pressure cooking, remember that for best results the pieces should be of equal size with the same

degree of ripeness. A small, ripe pear will fall apart before a larger, harder pear is cooked.

Purée
1. The trivet is not required when cooking fruit for a purée. In the open pressure cooker, dissolve 115g/4 oz sugar in the minimum recommended amount of water – usually 150ml/¼ pt or 300ml/½ pt (check in your instruction book).
2. Add the washed and roughly chopped fruit, making sure the pressure cooker is no more than half full (some fruit tends to froth up during pressure cooking).
3. Fit the lid and bring to pressure. Use High pressure for most fruit. Rhubarb and apple are best cooked at Medium pressure as they tend to froth during cooking. See the table on page 113 for cooking times.
4. Reduce the pressure slowly at room temperature.
5. Sieve the fruit or blend in a processor or liquidizer.

Soft fruit
Cooking in a container best retains the shape of more delicate soft fruit. You need add no liquid as it will produce its own concentrated juice. The container can be metal, ovenproof glass or china or boilable plastic. A soufflé dish is ideal as it can be used afterwards for serving at the table.

1. Arrange the washed and prepared fruit in layers in the container. Sprinkle sugar to taste between each layer. Cover securely with greaseproof paper or foil.
2. Put 300ml/½ pt water into the pressure cooker. Add the trivet and stand the container on it. Fit the lid and bring to High pressure. Follow the table for approximate cooking times (bear in mind that a china or glass dish will add 3–4 minutes on to the cooking time).
3. Reduce the pressure quickly in cold water.

Stone fruit

When cooking fruit with a stone, follow the method given for soft fruit. Either halve and stone the fruit or prick the skins twice with a fork.

Dried Fruit

1. Wash the fruit in hot water and place in a bowl. Cover with boiling water, allowing 600ml/1 pt for each 450g/ 1 lb fruit. Cover and leave to soak for 10 minutes.
2. Drain and measure the soaking water, making sure that you have at least 300ml/½ pt to pour into the pressure cooker, without the trivet. Add the fruit with 2–3 tablespoons sugar, or to taste.
3. Fit the lid and bring to High pressure. Follow the table for cooking times.
4. Reduce the pressure slowly at room temperature.

*Cooking times at High pressure for **dried fruit***	
Type of fruit	*Cooking time*
Apple rings	6 minutes
Apricots	4 minutes
Figs, pears, prunes	10 minutes
Peaches	5 minutes
Mixed Fruit	10 minutes

Steamed Puddings

Container

Use a heat resistant container, such as metal, boilable plastic, or ovenproof glass or china. Ensure that it is not too deep for your pressure cooker. Allow a gap of at least 5cm/2 in between the top of the basin and the lid to allow steam to circulate.

Timing
The cooking times given in the recipes and in the table are for puddings in metal or boilable plastic. When using ovenproof glass or china, add 10 minutes.

Basic Method
1. Grease the container and fill no more than three-quarters to allow room for the pudding to rise.
2. Cover the container with greased foil or a double thickness of greased greaseproof paper, tying it down securely.
3. Stand the container on the trivet in the pressure cooker and pour in the recommended amount of boiling water.
4. Fit the lid and heat until a thin jet of steam escapes from the vent in the lid. Reduce the heat so that the pudding steams gently, without reaching High pressure, for the recommended time, without the water boiling away furiously. It is during this steaming stage that the raising agent in the flour activates and the pudding rises.
5. At the end of the steaming time, bring to Low pressure and cook for the time recommended in the table.
6. Reduce the pressure slowly at room temperature to prevent the pudding from sinking. Remove the pudding using oven gloves.

Increasing Quantities
When increasing the quantities of a recipe, allow an extra 10 minutes' cooking time for every additional 55g/2 oz flour.

Adapting Steamed Pudding Recipes to Pressure Cooking			
Normal Cooking Time	*Water*	*Steaming*	*Pressure Cooking at Low*
30 minutes	850ml/1½ pt	5 minutes	10 minutes
1 hour	850ml/1½ pt	15 minutes	25 minutes
2–3 hours	1.2 litre/2 pt	20 minutes	1 hour

Cooking Times at High pressure for **Fresh Fruit**			
Type of Fruit	*Method*	*Purée*	*Container method*
Apples, sliced	For purée use Medium pressure	3 minutes	5–7 minutes
Apples, whole	See Apples with Honeyed Fruit, page 120	–	–
Apricots, halved	For container method, add 2 tbsp water	3 minutes	5–7 minutes
Blackberries		3 minutes	5–7 minutes
Blackcurrants		3 minutes	5–7 minutes
Cherries	For container method, cook whole with 2 tbsp water	–	5–7 minutes
Damsons	For container method, add 2 tbsp water	3 minutes	5–7 minutes
Gooseberries		3 minutes	5–7 minutes
Greengages	For container method, add 2 tbsp water	3 minutes	5–7 minutes
Loganberries		1 minute	4–6 minutes

Cooking Times at High pressure for **Fresh Fruit**			
Type of Fruit	Method	Purée	Container method
Pears	See Pears in Red Wine, page 119	3 minutes	–
Peaches, sliced		3 minutes	5–7 minutes
Peaches, halved	See Filled Peaches with Almonds, page 121	3 minutes	5–7 minutes
Plums	For container method, add 2 tbsp water	3 minutes	5–7 minutes
Raspberries		1 minute	4–6 minutes
Rhubarb	For purée use Medium pressure	1 minute	5–7 minutes

EGG CUSTARD

Serves 4   *10 minutes at High pressure*

This is such an easy dessert to make. I like it best served chilled with fresh or cooked fruit.

Butter
425ml/¾ pt milk
3 medium eggs
55g/2 oz caster sugar
½ tsp vanilla extract
Freshly ground nutmeg

1. Grease a 600ml/1 pt pudding basin or soufflé dish.

2. In a saucepan, gently heat the milk until warm but not hot.

3. In a bowl, lightly whisk the eggs with the sugar and vanilla.

4. Add the warm milk to the egg mixture and stir well.

5. Pour the custard mixture into the prepared dish. Sprinkle with a little nutmeg and cover securely with greaseproof paper or foil.

6. Put the trivet into the pressure cooker and stand the dish on top. Pour in 300ml/½ pt boiling water.

7. Fit the lid, bring to High pressure and cook for 10 minutes until set.

8. Reduce the pressure slowly at room temperature.

9. Carefully lift the dish from the pressure cooker, leave to cool and then chill.

CRÈME CARAMEL

Serves 4–6   *3 minutes at High pressure (individual)*
                      10 minutes at High pressure (large)

This is the dinner party version of egg custard and a favourite with most people. Make it in a large soufflé dish or in individual breakfast cups or moulds.

Butter

Caramel:
4 tbsp granulated sugar
4 tbsp water

Custard:
425ml/¾ pt milk
3 medium eggs
½ tsp vanilla extract
55g/2 oz caster sugar

1. Butter the dish(es).

2. Put the sugar into a thick-based saucepan over a low heat. With a wooden spoon, stir until the sugar has dissolved and turned a caramel colour.

3. Remove the pan from the heat and add the water all at once (do this quickly and carefully as the mixture may spit). Stir again over a gentle heat until the water has boiled and the caramel has dissolved. Pour into the dish(es) and swirl around to coat the base.

4. In a saucepan, gently heat the milk until warm but not hot.

5. In a bowl, lightly whisk the eggs with the sugar and vanilla.

6. Add the warm milk to the egg mixture and stir well.

7. Pour the custard mixture over the caramel in the dish(es). Cover securely with greaseproof paper or foil.

8. Put the trivet into the pressure cooker and stand the dish(es) on top. Pour in 300ml/½ pt boiling water.

9. Fit the lid, bring to High pressure and cook for 3 minutes (for individual dishes) or 10 minutes (for one large dish) until set.

10. Reduce the pressure slowly at room temperature.

11. Carefully lift the dish(es) out of the pressure cooker, leave to cool then chill overnight.

12. To serve, run the blade of a knife around the sides and turn out.

CREAMY CHOCOLATE POTS

Serves 4   *3 minutes at High pressure*

These make a delightful finish to an elegant meal.

115g/4 oz plain chocolate
3 medium egg yolks
25g/1 oz caster sugar
1 tbsp rum or orange liqueur
150ml/¼ pt milk
150ml/¼ pt double cream
Whipped cream, to decorate
Grated chocolate, to decorate

1. Break the chocolate into a basin and melt over a pan of hot water or on medium power in a microwave.

2. Beat in the egg yolks, sugar and rum or orange liqueur, mixing well.

3. Heat the milk in a saucepan (but do not allow it to boil) then stir into the chocolate mixture.

4. Strain the mixture into a jug for easy pouring and divide equally between four small ovenproof or ramekin dishes. Cover each one securely with greaseproof paper or foil.

5. Put the trivet into the pressure cooker with 300ml/½ pt water. Place the dishes on the trivet, ensuring that they do not touch the sides of the pressure cooker.

6. Fit the lid, bring to High pressure and cook for 3 minutes until set.

7. Reduce the pressure slowly at room temperature.

8. Leave to cool then chill until required. Serve decorated with whipped cream and chocolate.

PEARS IN RED WINE

Serves 4   *8 minutes at High pressure*

Serve just as they are or with a dollop of thick cream or crème
fraîche. The cooking time will depend on the ripeness of the
pears.

4 large firm pears
300ml/½ pt red wine
55g/2 oz caster sugar
¼ tsp ground cinnamon
Strip of lemon peel

1. Peel the pears, leaving the stalks intact. Shave a thin
    slice off the bottom of each pear so that it will stand
    upright.

2. Pour the wine into the pressure cooker, without the
    trivet, and add the sugar, cinnamon and lemon peel.

3. Heat gently, stirring continuously, until the sugar has
    dissolved.

4. Stand the pears upright in the pressure cooker, ensuring
    that they do not touch the sides. Spoon the liquid over
    the pears.

5. Fit the lid, bring to High pressure, cook for about 8
    minutes until the pears are soft.

6. Reduce the pressure quickly in cold water.

7. Using a spoon, lift the pears into a serving dish (don't be
    tempted to lift them by the stalks – they could break
    off). Pour the wine mixture over the pears.

8. Cool completely and chill before serving.

APPLES WITH HONEYED FRUIT

Serves 4   *4–6 minutes at High pressure*

Sometimes, I add some almond extract or ground mixed spice to the filling mixture in step 2.

4 cooking apples, washed and cored
140g/5 oz mixed dried fruit, such as sultanas and
   chopped apricots and cherries
2 tbsp honey
2 tbsp soft brown sugar

1. Grease four squares of foil and stand an apple in the centre of each.

2. Mix together the remaining ingredients and spoon into the apple centres (any left over can be put to the side of the apples). Crimp the foil at the edges to form a saucer shape.

3. Put the trivet into the pressure cooker with 300ml/½ pt water. Stand the apples and saucers on the trivet, ensuring that the apples do not touch the sides of the pressure cooker.

4. Fit the lid, bring to High pressure and cook for 4–6 minutes.

5. Reduce the pressure quickly in cold water.

6. Lift out the apples on their saucers and transfer to serving dishes, discarding the foil.

FILLED PEACHES WITH ALMONDS

Serves 4   *3 minutes at High pressure*

Serve these chilled, with cream or yoghurt drizzled over the top.

4 large firm peaches
25g/1 oz brown sugar
25g/1 oz soft butter
1 medium egg yolk
55g/2 oz digestive biscuits, crumbled
25g/1 oz chopped toasted almonds
25g/1 oz caster sugar
300ml/½ pt dry white wine
Toasted flaked almonds, to serve

1. To peel the peaches, put them in a bowl and pour over sufficient boiling water to cover. Leave to stand for 5 minutes, after which the skins should peel off easily. Halve each peach, removing the stones.

2. Combine the brown sugar and butter until well blended. Beat in the egg yolk and stir in the biscuit crumbs and chopped toasted almonds.

3. Spoon the mixture into the peach cavities.

4. Put the caster sugar and wine into the open pressure cooker, without the trivet, and heat gently until the sugar has dissolved. Stand the filled peach halves in the wine.

5. Fit the lid, bring to High pressure and cook for 3 minutes.

6. Reduce the pressure quickly in cold water.

7. Leave to cool and then chill until required. Serve sprinkled with toasted flaked almonds.

BREAD AND BUTTER PUDDING

Serves 2–3   *6 minutes at High pressure*

This old-fashioned favourite has become quite fashionable again! Make it into something special by varying your choice of bread (how about using a sweet bread such as brioche or croissants) and sprinkling the bread with a little of your favourite liqueur before cooking.

Butter
3 large slices of buttered bread, crusts removed if wished
55g/2 oz sultanas or chopped ready-to-eat dried fruit,
   such as apricots or dates
300ml/½ pt milk or milk and cream mixed
1 large egg, beaten
25g/1 oz caster sugar

1.   Butter a 600ml/1 pt ovenproof dish.

2.   Cut the bread into squares, arrange half over the base of the dish and sprinkle with half the fruit. Top with the remaining bread and fruit.

3.   Warm the milk (do not allow it to boil) and whisk into the egg and sugar. Pour the mixture over the bread and cover securely with greaseproof paper or foil. Leave to stand for about 15 minutes.

4.   Put 300ml/½ pt water into the pressure cooker with the trivet. Stand the dish on the trivet.

5.   Fit the lid, bring to pressure and cook for 6 minutes.

6.   Reduce the pressure slowly at room temperature.

7.   If wished, the top of the pudding can be lightly browned under a hot grill before serving.

ROLY POLY PUDDING

Serves 4–6   *20 minutes steaming*
                                    25 minutes at Low pressure

You could make this nursery pudding with jam in place of mincemeat. Either way, serve it in the traditional way – with plenty of creamy custard.

225g/8 oz self-raising flour
Pinch of salt
115g/4 oz shredded suet
About 300g/10½ oz mincemeat

1. Sift the flour and salt into a mixing bowl and stir in the suet. With a flat-blade knife, gradually stir in about 150ml/¼ pt cold water, using sufficient to make a soft, scone-like dough.

2. On a lightly floured surface, roll out the pastry thinly to make a rectangle (the short ends should be no wider than the diameter of your pressure cooker).

3. Spread the mincemeat over the pastry, leaving a narrow margin on all four edges. Dampen the pastry edges with water, roll up from the short end and crimp the ends.

4. Wrap loosely in buttered foil, sealing the packet securely.

5. Stand the pudding on the trivet in the pressure cooker and pour in 850ml/1½ pt boiling water.

6. Fit the lid and, without adding the weight or bringing to High pressure, gently steam over a low heat for 20 minutes.

7. Bring to Low pressure and cook for 25 minutes.

8. Reduce the pressure slowly at room temperature.

9. Remove the pudding carefully from the boiling water using two long-handled spoons.

10. Unwrap the pudding and serve it hot.

MIXED FRUIT PUDDING

Serves 6–8   *20 minutes steaming*
                                        45 minutes at Low pressure

You will probably find most of the ingredients for this pudding in your kitchen cupboards. The juice from the pineapple could be thickened with arrowroot and served as a sauce with the pudding.

115g/4 oz soft butter
115g/4 oz caster sugar
Finely grated rind and juice of 1 orange
2 medium eggs, lightly beaten
85g/3 oz self-raising flour
55g/2 oz fresh breadcrumbs
55g /2 oz glacé cherries
115g (4 oz) ready-to-eat dried fruit, (apricots, prunes, dates, figs), chopped
2 tbsp golden syrup or maple syrup
4 canned pineapple rings, drained

1.   Grease a 1.2 litre/2 pt pudding basin.

2.   Beat together the butter, sugar and orange rind until light and creamy. Gradually beat in the eggs. Combine the flour and breadcrumbs and fold into the mixture with the orange juice.

3.   Reserve two cherries. Chop the remainder and stir into the pudding mixture with the dried fruit.

4.   Spoon the syrup into the bottom of the basin.

5.   Arrange one pineapple slice on the base and the remainder around the sides. Halve the reserved cherries and place one half in the centre of each pineapple slice.

6.   Spoon the pudding mixture into the basin and cover securely with greased greaseproof paper or foil, folded

to allow the pudding to rise slightly. Stand the basin on the trivet in the pressure cooker.

7.   Fit the lid and, without adding the weight or bringing to High pressure, gently steam over a low heat for 20 minutes.

8.   Bring to Low pressure and cook for 45 minutes.

9.   Reduce the pressure slowly at room temperature.

10. Turn out onto a warmed plate to serve.

CHRISTMAS PUDDING

Makes a 675g/1½ lb pudding   *20 minutes steaming*
                                      2 hours at High pressure

Make your Christmas Pudding at least 4–6 weeks before Christmas and allow to mature in a cool place.

115g/4 oz butter, melted
115g/4 oz plain flour
115g/4 oz soft brown sugar
140g/5 oz currants
115g/4 oz raisins
85g/3 oz sultanas
25g/1 oz mixed peel
25g/1 oz blanched almonds, chopped
25g/1 oz glacé cherries, chopped
85g/3 oz fresh breadcrumbs
Finely grated rind of 1 small lemon
½ tsp grated nutmeg
2 tsp black treacle
1 large egg, beaten
1½ tbsp milk
1 tbsp rum

1. Put all the ingredients into a large bowl and mix well.

2. Spoon the mixture into a buttered 600ml/1 pt pudding basin and cover securely with a double layer of greased greaseproof paper.

3. Stand the basin on the trivet in the pressure cooker and pour in 1.7 litre/3 pt boiling water.

4. Fit the lid and, without adding the weight or bringing to High pressure, gently steam over a low heat for 20 minutes.

5. Bring to High pressure and cook for 2 hours.

6. Reduce the pressure slowly at room temperature.

7. Leave to cool completely, wrap in fresh greaseproof paper and store in a cool place until required.

8. To reheat, use the table below:

Cooking and reheating times for Christmas Puddings					
Weight of pudding	Basin capacity	Water	Steaming (minutes)	Cooking (hours)	Reheating (minutes)
450g/1 lb	600ml/1 pt	1.4 litre/2½ pt	15	1¾	20
675g/1½ lb	600ml/1 pt	1.7 litre/3 pt	20	2	30
900g/2 lb	1.2 litre/2 pt	2 litre/3½ pt	30	3	30

RHUBARB AND ORANGE PUDDING

Serves 4–6   *20 minutes steaming*
                                30 minutes at Low pressure

225g/8 oz self–raising flour
Pinch of salt
115g/4 oz shredded suet
675g/1½ lb rhubarb, cut into 2.5cm/1 inch pieces
175g/6 oz brown sugar
Finely grated rind and juice of 1 orange

1. Sift the flour and salt into a mixing bowl and stir in the suet. With a flat-blade knife, gradually stir in about 150ml/¼ pt cold water, using sufficient to make a soft, scone-like dough.

2. Reserve one third of the dough for the lid and roll the remaining dough into a circle, large enough to line a 1.2 litre/2 pt pudding basin. Grease the basin and line it with the pastry.

3. Fill the basin with layers of rhubarb, each sprinkled with sugar and orange rind. Pour the orange juice over.

4. Roll out the reserved pastry to make a lid, moisten the edges and crimp firmly into position, ensuring that there is space to allow the pastry to rise.

5. Cover securely with a double layer of greased grease-proof paper or a single layer of foil. Put the trivet and 1.5 litre/2¾ pt boiling water into the pressure cooker. Stand the basin on the trivet.

6. Fit the lid and, without adding the weight or bringing to High pressure, gently steam on a low heat for 20 minutes.

7. Bring to Low pressure and cook for 30 minutes.

8. Reduce the pressure slowly at room temperature.

9. Serve the pudding from the basin or turned out on to aserving dish.

CHOCOLATE SPONGE PUDDING

Serves 4   *20 minutes steaming*
25 minutes at Low pressure

Delightful served with chocolate sauce, custard or pouring cream.

55g/2 oz soft butter or margarine
55g/2 oz caster sugar
2 medium eggs, beaten
½ tsp vanilla extract
85g/3 oz self-raising flour
2 tbsp cocoa powder
Milk

1.   Beat together the butter and the sugar until light and fluffy. Beat in the eggs, a little at a time, and the vanilla extract. Sift over the flour and cocoa and fold into the mixture, adding sufficient milk to make a soft consistency.

2.   Spoon the mixture into a buttered 600ml/1 pt pudding basin and cover securely with greased greaseproof paper or foil.

3.   Stand the basin on the trivet in the pressure cooker and pour in 850ml/1½ pt boiling water.

4.   Fit the lid and, without adding the weight or bringing to High pressure, gently steam over a low heat for 20 minutes.

5.   Bring to Low pressure and cook for 25 minutes.

6.   Reduce the pressure slowly at room temperature.

7.   Turn out of the basin to serve.

GOLDEN SYRUP PUDDING

Serves 4   *20 minutes steaming*
                                     25 minutes at Low pressure

115g/4 oz self-raising flour
Pinch of salt
55g/2 oz shredded suet
55g/2 oz caster sugar
1 medium egg, beaten
2 tbsp milk
3 tbsp golden syrup

1. Sift the flour and salt into a mixing bowl and add the suet and sugar. Stir in the egg and milk to make a firm consistency.

2. Pour the syrup into a buttered 600ml/1 pt pudding basin and spoon the pudding mixture on top.

3. Cover securely with greased greaseproof paper or foil.

4. Stand the basin on the trivet in the pressure cooker and pour in 850ml/1½ pt boiling water.

5. Fit the lid and, without adding the weight or bringing to High pressure, gently steam over a low heat for 20 minutes.

6. Bring to Low pressure and cook for 25 minutes.

7. Reduce the pressure slowly at room temperature.

8. Turn out of the basin to serve.

RICE PUDDING

Serves 3–4   *12 minutes at High pressure*

This traditional dessert is quick to prepare in the pressure cooker.

25g/1 oz butter
600ml/1 pt milk
85g/3 oz pudding rice
55g/2 oz sugar
Freshly grated nutmeg

1. Melt the butter in the open pressure cooker, without the trivet, and swirl it round to coat the base.

2. Add the milk and, over medium heat, bring just to the boil. Add the rice and sugar and stir until the mixture just returns to the boil.

3. Reduce the heat until the milk simmers gently, fit the lid, bring slowly to High pressure and cook for 12 minutes.

4. Reduce the pressure slowly at room temperature.

5. Stir well and sprinkle with nutmeg. If wished, turn the pudding into a flameproof dish, sprinkle with nutmeg and brown for a few minutes under the grill.

7

COOKING FOR ONE

If you cook mostly for yourself, if you have limited cooking facilities, or if you are on a strict budget, it can be tempting to resort to the frying pan or to heating up ready meals.

In a pressure cooker, a main course and vegetables can be cooked together, with a dessert included for good measure. The secret is to choose food with similar cooking times or to adjust the preparation of food so that it all cooks in the same time.

For example, meat can often be the deciding factor in calculating the cooking time. If a chop takes 10 minutes, it's best to add root vegetables, which are unlikely to overcook in that time. Fish, on the other hand, takes less time, so accompanying potatoes would need to be thinly sliced in order to cook within the time. Frozen peas need only a couple of minutes and are best wrapped in foil to delay their cooking slightly.

I have assumed that anyone who cooks for one has probably purchased a smaller size of pressure cooker, which generally has a recommended minimum level of liquid of 150ml/¼ pt. But do check with your instruction book – if the manufacturer recommends a greater amount, you should increase accordingly the quantity specified in my recipes. This may mean increasing the amount of thickening at the end too.

COTTAGE PIE WITH CARROTS WITH CINNAMON AND GOOSEBERRIES

7 minutes at High pressure

You will need the trivet, two perforated baskets and one unperforated basket or basin.

1 tsp oil
175g/6 oz lean minced beef or lamb
1 baby onion or shallot, finely chopped
Salt and freshly ground black pepper
1 tsp Worcestershire sauce
150ml/¼ pt beef, lamb or vegetable stock
2 medium potatoes, thinly sliced
4 small carrots, sliced
Butter
115g/4 oz fresh or frozen gooseberries
25g/1 oz sugar
Pinch of ground cinnamon
1 tbsp cornflour
Crisp sweet biscuits, to serve

1.   Heat the oil in the open pressure cooker, add the mince and onion and cook, stirring occasionally, until browned. Season with salt and pepper. Add the Worcestershire sauce and the stock.

2.   Put the potatoes and carrots into the two perforated baskets and season lightly.

3.   Butter the unperforated basket or basin and add the gooseberries. Combine the sugar and cinnamon and sprinkle over the fruit. Add 2 tbsp water and cover securely with foil.

4.   Place the trivet on top of the meat in the pressure cooker and stand the three containers on top.

5.   Fit the lid, bring to High pressure and cook for 7 minutes.

6.   Reduce the pressure quickly in cold water.

7.   Lift out the three containers.

8.   Blend the cornflour with 1 tbsp cold water to make a smooth paste and stir into the meat in the pressure cooker. Cook, stirring, until the mixture comes to the boil and thickens. Adjust the seasoning to taste.

9.   Spoon the meat into an oven-proof dish, cover with the sliced potatoes and brown under a hot grill. Alternatively, spoon the meat on to a warm plate and top with the potatoes. Serve with the carrots, dotted with butter if wished.

10. Serve the gooseberries warm or cold with crisp biscuits.

LAMB AND APRICOT CURRY AND RICE WITH BAKED APPLE

10 minutes at High pressure

You will need the trivet and an unperforated basket or basin.

55g/2 oz basmati or long grain rice
1 cooking apple or 1 large eating apple, cored
1 tsp brown sugar
1 tsp honey
2 tsp sultanas
2 tsp oil
2 lean lamb chops
1 baby onion or shallot
2 tsp curry powder or 1 tsp curry paste
150ml/¼ pt lamb or vegetable stock
40g/1½ oz ready-to-eat dried apricots, roughly chopped
1 tsp mango chutney
1 tbsp tomato purée
1 tbsp cornflour
1 tbsp lemon juice
Chopped fresh coriander, to serve
Toasted flaked almonds, to serve
Cream or thick yoghurt, to serve

1. Put the rice into the unperforated basket and pour over 100ml/3½ fl oz lightly salted water. Cover securely with foil.

2. With a sharp knife, score a ring in the skin around the centre of the apple. Stand it on a large piece of buttered foil. Combine the sugar, honey and sultanas and spoon the mixture into the centre of the apple. Fold the foil over to make a parcel and seal securely.

3. Heat the oil in the open pressure cooker, add the lamb chops and brown quickly on both sides. Add the onion and

curry powder or paste and cook, stirring for 1–2 minutes. Add the stock, apricots, chutney and tomato purée.

4. Place the trivet on top of the meat in the pressure cooker and stand the container of rice and wrapped apple on top.

5. Fit the lid, bring to High pressure and cook for 10 minutes.

6. Reduce the pressure quickly in cold water.

7. Lift out the container and the apple, leaving them covered.

8. Blend the cornflour with the lemon juice to make a smooth paste and add to the lamb. Cook, stirring, until the mixture comes to the boil and thickens.

9. Uncover the rice and fluff up with a fork to separate the grains. Serve with the curry spooned over and topped with coriander and almonds.

10. Serve the apple with cream or yoghurt.

ITALIAN-STYLE PORK WITH POTATO, PARSNIP AND HERB MASH WITH CARIBBEAN BANANA

10 minutes at High pressure

You will need the trivet, two perforated separator baskets and a buttered square of foil.

25g/1 oz raisins
1 tbsp rum
15g/½ oz butter, plus extra for mash
1 lean pork chop
2 baby onions or shallots, finely chopped
1 small red pepper, seeds removed and sliced
227g can chopped tomatoes
Salt and freshly ground black pepper
Pinch of rosemary
2–3 small potatoes, halved
2 medium parsnips, thickly sliced
1 banana, peeled
1 tsp golden syrup
1 tbsp chopped fresh herbs, such as coriander or parsley

1. Put the raisins and rum into a cup and leave to soak while you prepare the rest of the meal.

2. Heat the butter in the open pressure cooker, add the pork and brown quickly on both sides. Add the onions and pepper, tomatoes, seasoning and rosemary.

3. Put the potatoes and parsnips into the two separators and season.

4. Place the trivet on top of the meat and stand the separators on the trivet.

5. Put the banana on to a square of foil and fold the sides up. Pour over the syrup, raisins and rum. Fold the foil

over the banana to form a secure parcel. Place it on the trivet.

6. Fit the lid, bring to High pressure and cook for 10 minutes.

7. Reduce the pressure quickly in cold water.

8. Mash the potatoes with the parsnips, stirring in the herbs and butter to taste.

9. Serve the mash with the chop and the tomato sauce spooned over.

10. Unwrap the banana carefully and serve with the sauce spooned over.

BEEF AND VEGETABLE CASSEROLE WITH BREAD AND BUTTER PUDDING

15 minutes at High pressure

You will need the trivet and a greased unperforated separator basket or small pudding basin.

1 tbsp oil
1 small onion, finely chopped
175g/6 oz lean stewing steak, cut into cubes
2 small potatoes, sliced
2 small carrots, cut into small dice
1 medium parsnip, cut into small dice
Salt and freshly ground black pepper
150ml/¼ pt beef or vegetable stock
2 tsp Worcestershire sauce
2 slices of bread, buttered and cut into squares
1 tbsp dried fruit, such as cherries, cranberries or sultanas
1 tsp caster sugar
1 medium egg, beaten
150ml/¼ pt full cream milk, warmed if possible
Pinch of grated nutmeg
Cornflour (optional)

1. Heat the oil in the open pressure cooker, add the onion and cook gently, stirring occasionally, until softened but not browned. Add the steak and brown quickly on all sides. Add the remaining vegetables, seasoning, stock and Worcestershire sauce. Place the trivet on top of the stew.

2. In an unperforated separator basket or small pudding basin, layer the bread with the fruit and sugar. Mix together the egg and milk and pour over the bread. Sprinkle with nutmeg and cover securely with foil.

3.   Stand the container on the trivet in the centre of the pressure cooker.

4.   Fit the lid, bring to High pressure and cook for 15 minutes.

5.   Reduce the pressure slowly at room temperature.

6.   Lift out the pudding and turn out on to a serving dish.

7.   If wished, thicken the stew by blending some cornflour with a little water to make a smooth paste, stirring in and bringing to the boil, stirring, until thickened.

8

PRESERVES

A pressure cooker can be used for making jam, marmalade, conserves or curds, or for bottling fruit.

In jam making, pressure cooking speeds up the softening of the fruit and, since little liquid is added, the flavour is more concentrated and setting point is achieved more quickly.

A pressure cooker also offers a quicker and therefore cheaper alternative to oven bottling.

Jam Making
The success of the jam depends on using good quality, undamaged fruit. Berry fruits such as raspberries and strawberries do not require softening under pressure but the open

pressure cooker may be used as a large pan to prepare the jam in the traditional way.

1. The trivet is not used.
2. The softening stage releases the pectin from the fruit so that the jam will eventually set. Put the water and fruit into the pressure cooker, making sure that it is no more than half full. Fit the lid, bring to Medium pressure and cook for up to 5 minutes, depending on the ripeness of the fruit and its type. Reduce the pressure slowly at room temperature.
3. Put the clean, dry jam-jars to warm in a low oven.
4. Calculate the amount of sugar required. This will be approximately equal to the weight of the fruit. Warm the sugar slightly in a bowl in a low oven as this helps it to dissolve quickly to give good colour and flavour.
5. Add the sugar and cook over a low heat, stirring continuously until dissolved. Do not fit the lid once the sugar has been added.
6. Bring to the boil and boil rapidly until the jam reaches setting point. You can gauge this most accurately with a sugar thermometer as setting occurs at 104°C/221°F. Alternatively, stir the jam with a wooden spoon, cool the spoon slightly and, if the jam partly gels, setting point has been reached. A third method is to remove the pressure cooker from the heat and spoon a little jam on to a cold saucer. Leave it to cool, then rub your finger over the surface – if it wrinkles, the jam is ready to set.
7. As soon as the jam reaches setting point, remove the pressure cooker from the heat.
8. Remove any scum and ladle the jam into a heatproof jug (I find it easier to pour the jam into the jars rather than use a ladle). Stand the jars on newspaper (to help prevent them cracking). Fill, cover with waxed discs and, when cool, cover and label.

APRICOT JAM

Makes about 2.25kg/5 lb   *10 minutes at High pressure*

A jam for making at any time of the year.

450g/1 lb dried apricots, chopped
Juice of 1 lemon
1.3kg/3 lb preserving sugar

1.   Put the apricots into the pressure cooker without the trivet. Cover with 1.2 litre/2 pt boiling water and leave to soak for 10 minutes.

2.   Add the lemon juice.

3.   Fit the lid, bring to High pressure and cook for 10 minutes.

4.   Reduce the pressure slowly at room temperature.

5.   Add the sugar and heat gently, stirring, until dissolved.

6.   Increase the heat and boil rapidly in the open pan until the jam reaches setting point. Skim if necessary.

7.   Cool the jam slightly until a skin forms (this helps to prevent the fruit rising in the jars) then pour into warmed, dry jars. Cover and label.

DAMSON JAM

Makes about 2.25kg/5 lb   5 minutes at Medium pressure

This works well with plums too.

1.25kg/2¾ lb damsons, washed
1.3kg/3 lb granulated sugar

1. Put the damsons into the pressure cooker without the trivet. Add 300ml/½ pt water.

2. Fit the lid, bring to Medium pressure and cook for 5 minutes.

3. Reduce the pressure slowly at room temperature.

4. Add the sugar and heat gently, stirring, until dissolved.

5. Increase the heat and boil rapidly in the open pan until the jam reaches setting point. Skim if necessary.

6. Cool the jam slightly until a skin forms (this helps to prevent the fruit rising in the jars) then pour into warmed, dry jars. Cover and label.

ORANGE MARMALADE

Makes about 2.25kg/5 lb   10–15 minutes at High pressure

Seville oranges are available in January. I like to buy them and pop them in the freezer until I am ready to make the marmalade.

675g/1½ lb Seville oranges, washed and halved
Juice of 1 large or 2 small lemons
1.3kg/3 lb granulated sugar

1. Squeeze the juice from the oranges and tie the pith and pips in muslin. Cut the peel as thinly as preferred. Soak the peel and muslin bag in 600ml/1 pt water for several hours or overnight.

2. Put the orange juice and lemon juice into the pressure cooker without the trivet. Add the water, peel and muslin bag.

3. Fit the lid, bring to High pressure and cook for 10–15 minutes depending on the thickness of the peel.

4. Reduce the pressure slowly at room temperature.

5. Using two spoons, squeeze the juice from the muslin bag into the pressure cooker, then discard the bag.

6. Add the sugar and heat gently, stirring, until dissolved.

7. Increase the heat and boil rapidly in the open pan until the marmalade reaches setting point. Skim if necessary.

8. Cool the marmalade slightly until a skin forms (this helps to prevent the fruit rising in the jars) then pour into warmed, dry jars. Cover and label.

GOOSEBERRY AND GINGER JAM

Makes about 2.25kg/5 lb   *3 minutes at Medium pressure*

Ginger complements gooseberries beautifully.

1.3kg/3 lb gooseberries, topped and tailed
55g/2 oz crystallised ginger, finely chopped
1.3kg/3 lb sugar

1.   Put the gooseberries and ginger into the pressure cooker without the trivet. Add 300ml/½ pt water.

2.   Fit the lid, bring to Medium pressure and cook for 3 minutes.

3.   Reduce the pressure slowly at room temperature.

4.   Add the sugar and heat gently, stirring, until dissolved.

5.   Increase the heat and boil rapidly in the open pan until the jam reaches setting point. Skim if necessary.

6.   Cool the jam slightly until a skin forms (this helps to prevent the fruit rising in the jars) then pour into warmed, dry jars. Cover and label.

APPLE JELLY

3 minutes at Medium pressure

A great way to use windfalls.

1.3kg/3 lb cooking apples, washed
Juice of 1 lemon
Granulated sugar

1. Trim the apples of any bruised areas. Slice thickly without peeling or removing the core.

2. Put the apples and lemon juice into the pressure cooker without the trivet. Add 300ml/½ pt water.

3. Fit the lid, bring to Medium pressure and cook for 3 minutes.

4. Reduce the pressure slowly at room temperature.

5. Mash the fruit and leave it to strain through a jelly bag or clean tea towel into a bowl (don't be tempted to squeeze the bag to speed up the process as this will make the jelly cloudy).

6. Measure the liquid and weigh 450g/1 lb sugar for each 600ml/1 pt juice.

7. Return the juice to the clean pressure cooker.

8. Add the sugar and heat gently, stirring, until dissolved.

9. Increase the heat and boil rapidly in the open pan until the jelly reaches setting point. Skim if necessary.

10. Cool the jelly slightly until a skin forms (this helps to prevent the fruit rising in the jars) then pour into warmed, dry jars. Cover and label.

REDCURRANT JELLY

1 minute at Medium pressure

Enjoy the fresh taste of summer throughout the year.

1.3kg/3 lb redcurrants, washed with stalks intact
Granulated sugar

1. Put the redcurrants (stalks and all) into the pressure cooker without the trivet. Add 300ml/½ pt water.

2. Fit the lid, bring to Medium pressure and cook for 3 minutes.

3. Reduce the pressure slowly at room temperature.

4. Mash the fruit and leave it to strain through a jelly bag or clean tea towel into a bowl (don't be tempted to squeeze the bag to speed up the process as this will make the jelly cloudy).

5. Measure the liquid and weigh 550g/1¼ lb sugar for each 600ml/1 pt juice.

6. Return the juice to the clean pressure cooker.

7. Add the sugar and heat gently, stirring, until dissolved.

8. Increase the heat and boil rapidly in the open pan until the jelly reaches setting point. Skim if necessary.

9. Cool the jelly slightly until a skin forms (this helps to prevent the fruit rising in the jars) then pour into warmed, dry jars. Cover and label.

LEMON CURD

Makes about 900g/2 lb   *10 minutes at High pressure*

Nothings compares with the sparkling fresh flavour of home-made lemon curd. Store it in the refrigerator and use within 6 weeks.

4 large eggs, beaten
450g/1 lb caster sugar
Finely grated rind of 4 lemons
Strained juice of 2 lemons
85g/3 oz butter, cut into small cubes

1. Strain the eggs into a heat-resistant bowl and stir in the sugar. Add the lemon rind, juice and butter. Cover securely with greased greaseproof paper.

2. Pour 300ml/½ pt water into the pressure cooker and add the trivet. Stand the bowl on the trivet.

3. Fit the lid, bring to High pressure and cook for 10 minutes.

4. Reduce the pressure slowly at room temperature.

5. Lift the basin from the pressure cooker, remove the cover and, with a wooden spoon, stir until well blended.

6. Pour into warmed, dry jars, cover and label.

GREEN TOMATO CHUTNEY

Makes about 1.3kg/3 lb   *10 minutes at High pressure*

All gardeners need a recipe to use up unripened tomatoes and
windfall apples!

425ml/¾ pt malt vinegar
1.3kg/3 lb green tomatoes, thinly sliced
3 onions, finely chopped
3 cooking apples, peeled, cored and finely chopped
175g/6 oz sultanas
2 tsp salt
3 tsp pickling spice, tied in muslin
250g/9 oz soft brown sugar

1. Put half the vinegar into the pressure cooker without the
   trivet. Add the remaining ingredients except for the
   sugar.

2. Fit the lid, bring to High pressure and cook for 10
   minutes.

3. Reduce the pressure quickly in cold water.

4. Stir in the remaining vinegar and the sugar.

5. Bring to the boil in the open pan and simmer over a low
   heat, stirring occasionally, until the chutney thickens.

6. Remove the spice bag.

7. Pour the chutney into warmed, dry jars, cover and label.

APPLE CHUTNEY

Makes about 1.8kg/4 lb   *12 minutes at Medium pressure*

This is delicious served with cold meats and pork in particular.
It's good on a "ploughman's" too.

300ml/½ pt malt vinegar
1.3kg/3 lb cooking apples, peeled, cored and diced
450g/1 lb onions, finely chopped
225g/8 oz sultanas
1 tsp salt
Pinch of cayenne pepper
675g/1½ lb brown sugar

1. Put the vinegar into the pressure cooker without the trivet. Add the remaining ingredients except for the sugar.

2. Fit the lid, bring to Medium pressure and cook for 12 minutes.

3. Reduce the pressure quickly in cold water.

4. Stir in the sugar.

5. Bring to the boil in the open pan and simmer over a low heat, stirring occasionally, until the chutney thickens.

6. Remove the spice bag.

7. Pour the chutney into warmed, dry jars, cover and label.

Fruit Bottling

Choose firm, unblemished fruit of equal size and ripeness to ensure even cooking. Fruit such as apple, which discolours when peeled, should be covered in a solution of 1 teaspoon salt to 600ml/1 pt water until ready for bottling. Rinse well in cold water before packing the apple into the bottles.

Hard fruit, such as apples and pears, need slight cooking before bottling. Put 300ml/½ pt water into the pressure cooker with the trivet and pile the fruit on the trivet, making sure that the pressure cooker is no more than half full. Fit the lid and bring to High pressure. Reduce the pressure immediately in cold water to avoid overcooking.

As soft fruits, such as raspberries and strawberries, tend to shrink when cooked, it is best to soak them overnight in a heavy syrup before bottling.

Fruit bottled in a syrup will give better results in terms of flavour and colour but water can be used instead. When making the syrup, boil granulated sugar in water for about a minute. If you prefer a light syrup, use 55–115g/2–4 oz sugar for each 600ml/1 pt water. For a heavier syrup for desserts, use 175–225g/6–8 oz for each 600ml/1 pt water. When bottling fruit, use Low pressure.

Method

1. Immerse the clean jars and lids in boiling water while preparing the fruit.
2. Pack the cleaned fruit into the jars. Pack tightly to the shoulder of the jar.
3. Bring to the boil the prepared syrup and, using a jug, pour into the jars, a little at a time, releasing any air bubbles by tapping the jar gently against a board. Leave a space at the top of about 5mm/¼ in.
4. Fit the rubber bands and tops. If the jars are sealed by metal clips, these should be fitted at this stage, but if metal screw bands are used, they should be screwed down until tight, then unscrewed for a quarter turn. This is to allow air and steam to escape from the jars during bottling. Return the jars to the hot water.

5. Put the trivet into the pressure cooker upside down and pour in 1.2 litre/2 pt boiling water. Stand the jars in the pressure cooker, making sure that they don't touch each other or the sides of the pressure cooker (otherwise they could crack).
6. Using a medium heat bring to Low pressure and cook for the time recommended in the following table. Reduce pressure slowly at room temperature.
7. Remove the jars and screw tight the jars fitted with metal screw bands. Metal clips tighten automatically.
8. Test the seal the next day by unscrewing the bands or removing the clips. If the covers remain firmly in position, label the jars and store. If they can be removed, the fruit should be used as soon as possible and you should examine the bottle, cover, seal and band or clip as one of them could be faulty.

Fruit	Minutes at Low pressure
Apple, thickly sliced	1
Apricots, halved and stoned	1
Blackberries	1
Cherries	1
Damsons	1
Gooseberries (only when firm)	1
Greengages	1
Loganberries	3
Peaches, skinned and halved	1
Pears, halved or quartered	3
Pineapple, cubed	3
Plums, whole or halved	1
Raspberries	1
Rhubarb	2
Strawberries	3

INDEX

A

Adapting recipes for pressure cooking, 17, 20
American-style butter beans, 102
Apple with honeyed fruit, 120
, baked, 136
chutney, 153
jelly, 149
Apricot jam, 145

B

Bacon and beans, 57
, boiled, 58
in cider, 59
Baked apple, 136
Banana, Caribbean, 138
Barbecue-style spare ribs, 54
Baskets, 12
Beef and vegetable casserole, 140
, curried, 48
goulash, 47
in brown ale, 49
pot roast, 53
with vegetables, 46
Blanching vegetables, 95
Boiled bacon, 58
Bolognese sauce, 52
Bottling, fruit, 154
Braising fish, 83
Bread and butter pudding, 122, 140
Broad bean and bacon soup, 28
Butter beans, American-style, 102

C

Cabbage in a creamy sauce, 101
with apple, red, 103
Caribbean banana, 138
Carrot and orange soup, 32
Casserole, beef and vegetable, 140
, Devon fish, 87
, leek and tomato, 106
Casseroling fish, 83
Celery soup, 25
Chicken and herbs, rice with, 74
and mushroom soup, 42
and pineapple curry, 69
in a cream sauce, 77
liver pâté, 68
marengo, 75
pot roast, 70
soup, 40
with cashew nuts, spiced, 76
with summer vegetables, 71
with tarragon and lemon, 69
Christmas pudding, 126
Chocolate pots, creamy, 118
sponge pudding, 129
Chutney, apple, 153
, green tomato, 152
Cock-a-leekie soup, 39
Cod Provençal, 86
Cooking times for bottled fruit, 156
fish, 84
fruit, 110–111
jams, 144
puddings, 112–114
rice, 93–94

single servings, 132–133
soup, 21
meat, 44
poultry and game, 66–67
vegetables, 94, 96–99
Coq au vin, 72
Cottage pie with carrots, 134
Country liver pâté
Courgettes, Provençal style, 108
Creamy chocolate pots, 118
Créme caramel, 116
Curried beef, 48
Curry, Chicken and pineapple, 69
, lamb and apricot, 136

D
Damson jam, 146
Devon fish casserole, 87
lamb and potato pie, 60

E
Egg custard, 115

F
Filled peaches with almonds, 121
peppers, 105
Fish, 81 *et seq*
, braising, 83
casserole, Devon, 87
en papillote, 82–83
in caper sauce, white, 91
, poaching, 82
, steaming, 82
, stewing, 83
stock, 35
soup, Mediterranean, 36
Fixed pressure, 10
Freezing fish, 84
meat, 45
poultry and game, 66
soup, 20–21
vegetables, 96
Fruit bottling, 154
, dried, 111
, fresh, 109–111

G
Game, 65 *et seq*
Golden syrup pudding, 130
Gooseberry and ginger jam, 148

Green lentils with pancetta and
mustard, 104
tomato chutney, 152

H
High pressure, 10
Herrings, soused, 90
Hotpot, Lancashire, 61

I
Italian-style pork, 138

J
Jam, apricot, 145
, damson, 146
, gooseberry and ginger, 148
making, 143–144
Jelly, apple, 149
, redcurrant, 150

K
Kedgeree, smoked mackerel, 85

L
Lamb and apricot curry, 136
and potato pie, Devon, 60
with cinnamon and apricots, 62
Lancashire hotpot, 61
Lemon curd, 151
Lentil soup, 33
Lentils with pancetta and mustard,
green, 104
Leek and tomato casserole, 106
Lettuce soup, 23
Liquid levels, 13, 44
Liver and onions, 63
Looking after a pressure cooker, 16–17
Low pressure, 10

M
Mackerel with gooseberry sauce, 92
Marmalade, orange, 147
Meat, 43 *et seq*
Medium pressure, 10
Minestrone soup, 29
Mixed fruit pudding, 125
Mulligatawny soup, 38

O
One, cooking for, 133 *et seq*
Onion soup, french, 31
Orange marmalade, 147

P

Pâté, country liver, 64
Peaches with almonds, filled, 121
Pears in red wine, 119
Peppers, filled, 105
Pheasant with grapes, 80
Pie, cottage, 135
    lamb and potato, 60
Poaching fish, 82
Pork, Italian-style, 138
    , sweet and sour, 55
    with lemon and olives, 56
Pot roast, chicken, 70
    , beef, 53
Poultry, 65 et seq
Preserves, 143 et seq
Pressure, high, 10
    indicator, audible, 14–15
    indicator, visual, 13–14
    , low, 10
    , medium, 10
    valve, fixed, 15
Provençal style, courgettes, 108
Pudding, bread and butter, 122, 140
    , chocolate sponge, 129
    , Christmas, 126
    , golden syrup, 130
    , mixed fruit, 124
    , rhubarb and orange, 128
    , rice, 131
    , roly poly, 123
    , salmon, 88
Puddings, 109 et seq
Purée fruit, 110

R

Rack, 11
Ragoût of venison, 78
Ratatouille, 100
Red cabbage with apple, 103
Redcurrant jelly, 150
Reducing pressure, 16
Reheating frozen meat, 45
Rhubarb and orange pudding, 128
Rice, 93 et seq
    pudding, 131
    with chicken and herbs, 74
'Risotto' with courgettes, 107
Roly poly pudding, 123

S

Safety, 7, 12
Salmon pudding, 88
Scotch broth, 37
Seasoning soups, 20
Smoked mackerel kedgeree, 85
Soup, 19 et seq
    , broad bean and bacon, 28
    , carrot and orange, 32
    , celery, 25
    , chicken and mushroom, 42
    , cock-a-leekie, 39
    , chicken, 40
    , french onion, 31
    , fresh tomato, 26
    , lentil, 33
    , lettuce, 23
    , Mediterranean fish, 36
    , minestrone, 29
    , mixed vegetable, 30
    , mulligatawny, 38
    , split pea and bacon, 34
    , vichyssoise, 27
    , watercress, 24
Spare ribs, barbecue-style, 54
Spiced chicken with cashew nuts, 76
Split pea and bacon soup, 34
Steak and kidney pudding, 51
Steaming fish, 82
Stewing fish, 83
Stock, 22
    , fish, 35
Soused herrings, 90
Sweet and sour pork, 55

T

Thickening meat dishes, 44
    soup, 20
Tomato soup, fresh, 26
Trivet, 11
Trout with buttery almonds, 89

V

Vegetable soup, mixed, 30
Vegetables, 93 et seq
Venison, ragoût of, 78
Vichyssoise, 27

W

Watercress soup, 24
White fish in caper sauce, 91

RIGHT WAY
PUBLISHING POLICY

HOW WE SELECT TITLES

RIGHT WAY consider carefully every deserving manuscript. Where an author is an authority on his subject but an inexperienced writer, we provide first-class editorial help. The standards we set make sure that every **RIGHT WAY** book is practical, easy to understand, concise, informative and delightful to read. Our specialist artists are skilled at creating simple illustrations which augment the text wherever necessary.

CONSISTENT QUALITY

At every reprint our books are updated where appropriate, giving our authors the opportunity to include new information.

FAST DELIVERY

We sell **RIGHT WAY** books to the best bookshops throughout the world. It may be that your bookseller has run out of stock of a particular title. If so, he can order more from us at any time – we have a fine reputation for ''same day'' despatch, and we supply any order, however small (even a single copy), to any bookseller who has an account with us. We prefer you to buy from your bookseller, as this reminds him of the strong underlying public demand for **RIGHT WAY** books. However, you can order direct from us by post, by phone with a credit card, or through our web site.

FREE

If you would like an up-to-date list of all **RIGHT WAY** titles currently available, please send a stamped self-addressed envelope to

ELLIOT RIGHT WAY BOOKS,
BRIGHTON ROAD, LOWER KINGSWOOD,
TADWORTH, SURREY, KT20 6TD, U.K.

or visit our web site at www.right-way.co.uk